And Now for the Good News

Thanks for helping spread the good news!

Sue Ray

And Now for the Good News

a mega-dose of positive news to inform,
inspire, and fill you with optimism

---

*reporting and resources
presented by Sue Ray*

Moment Point Press
Needham, Massachusetts

Moment Point Press
PO Box 920287
Needham, MA 02492

Neither the author nor the publisher has received any compensation whatsoever from any of the individuals, businesses, or organizations featured in this book.

Library of Congress Cataloging-in-Publication Data
Ray, Sue
    And now for the good news : a mega-dose of positive news to inform, inspire, and fill you with optimism / reporting and resources presented by Sue Ray.
    p. cm.
    ISBN 978-1-930491-13-7 (pbk. : alk. paper) 1. United States—Social life and customs—1971—Anecdotes. 2. United States—Social conditions—1980—Anecdotes. 3. United States—Economic conditions—1980—Anecdotes. 4. Youth—United States—Social conditions—Anecdotes. 5. Social history—1970—Anecdotes. 6. Economic history—1990—Anecdotes. 7. Sustainable development—Anecdotes. 8. Environmental protection—Anecdotes. 9. Social values—Anecdotes. 10. Optimism—Miscellanea.
    I. Title.
    E169.Z83R395 2007
    973.924–dc22   2007019161

Cover and text design: Kathryn Sky-Peck
Typesetting: Phillip Augusta
Printing: McNaughton & Gunn

First printing June 2007
ISBN 978-1-930491-13-7

Printed in the United States on acid-free, partially recycled paper.
Distributed to the trade by Red Wheel Weiser

10 9 8 7 6 5 4 3 2 1

To Mathew, my very own daily dose of good news

Contents

Charity by the numbers . . . Living in a state of
generosity . . . *Focus-Worthy Resource:* Before you
write that generous check . . . Women's group discovers
giving never tasted so good . . . *May I Suggest:* Fun
and easy ways to develop your child's anterior
prefrontal cortex . . . One woman's determination
illustrates that we can always make a difference . . .
One man's generosity and forethought keep him alive
for posterity . . . Where have all the billionaires gone?
. . . Three news stories remind us that to err is human
and to forgive is, too . . . *Focus-Worthy Resource:* A
magazine for intelligent optimists

We're not only living longer, we're living longer better . . . The placebo effect confounds researchers and points to the healing power of belief . . . West meets east and changes the face of mainstream medicine . . . Have a good laugh, meditate, you'll live forever . . . Reality struts her stuff down the runway . . . Our kids got too big for their britches, now we're helping them slim down and get healthy . . . A California middle school transforms an acre of unused land into a world of healthy learning . . . A Baltimore school lets kids prove to themselves that getting fit is just plain fun

More U.S. teens are saying nope to dope . . . High school students are making brighter choices . . . One school gets big results with three new Rs: resources, responsibility, and real-world experience . . . Girls take top prizes at the international science and engineering fair, again . . . *May I Suggest*: Serving up some good news at dinnertime . . . A student and a city remind us that kids are both resourceful and resources . . . *Focus-Worthy Resource*: Youth connecting with youth to get things done . . . College students may not have a lot of cash to spare, but they've been giving their time in record numbers

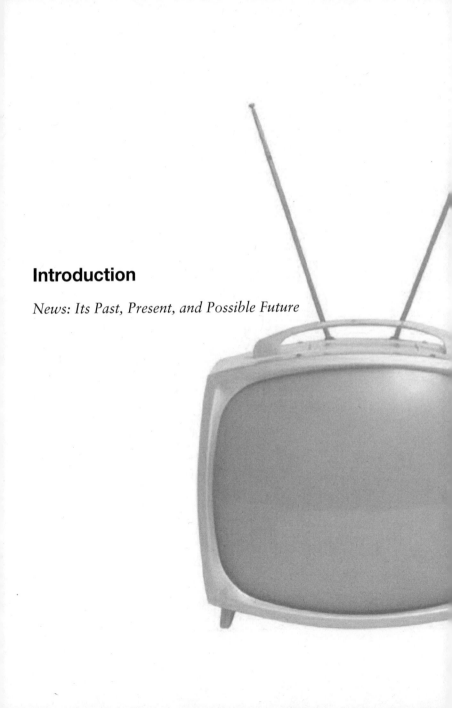

Introduction

News: Its Past, Present, and Possible Future

news

noun / plural but singular in construction

a report of recent events • previously unknown information •
newly received or noteworthy information, especially about
recent and important events • a presentation or broadcast of
newsworthy material

"Recent events," "previously unknown information," "news-worthy," so says the dictionary definition, but we all know "news" really means "mostly bad news." Whether TV, radio, Internet, or newspaper be the source, the daily headlines are a catalog of natural disasters and human misbehavior, greed, deceit, and downright cruelty.

Glance through the table of contents of nearly any newspaper or news magazine and we're hard pressed to find a feature story that could be considered positive, while Internet news sites, most being the off-shoots of print and TV media outlets, simply recycle the same negative stories we see in print and on TV. When there *is* something positive reported in the mainstream media, it's nearly always relegated to an end-of-the-show, or even end-of-the-week segment, and tends to be simply feel-good rather than truly informative. We're all familiar with the TV-news lead-in formula:

"Tonight: A man beats his neighbor senseless over a property-line dispute. Scientists warn that none of us are safe from a newly discovered virus. A government persecutes its own people." Slight pause, news anchor breaks into a half-smile. "And a dog saves the life of his owner by dialing 911."

When important good news *is* reported, it usually gets one airing, from one angle. Unlike, say, the coverage of the Enron scandal, the Scooter Libby trial, or the life and death of Anna Nicole Smith, which get continuous coverage, for weeks, sometimes months, until we're left with the impression that all corporations and politicians are greedy and corrupt, all celebrities lead lives of ridiculous excess and bad choices—and there's no other news in the world worthy of reporting.

It's enough to leave one feeling hopeless.

Positive psychologist and best-selling author Martin Seligman says we're a nation in depression. "We are in the middle of an epidemic," he says. "Severe depression is ten times more prevalent today than it was fifty years ago" (*Learned Optimism*, Vintage, 2006).

It makes you wonder—could it be we're more depressed today because we receive more bad news each day than at any time in our history? After all, similar to the way we've supersized our cars, our meals, and our homes, we've supersized our news.

Fifty years ago, before the days of cable TV and the Internet, the average person received news from either a daily paper or from one of the Big Three TV networks' nightly news programs, which were 15 minutes long. That's right, when Chet Huntley teamed up with David Brinkley in 1956 for NBC's hugely popular evening news broadcast, *The Huntley-Brinkley Report*, they covered politics and global issues for *15 minutes*. They didn't increase to a half hour until 1963, following CBS's lead. ABC also followed suit.

The *big* change didn't happen until 17 years later, in 1980, when entrepreneur Ted Turner founded CNN, the Cable News Network. Suddenly, the news was on 24 hours a day, seven days a week. As a result, by the late 1980s, the Big Three, scrambling to compete, expanded their news offerings to morning, noon, and night. And to fill up all that time—the same stories and images started getting repeated over and over and . . .

Cable news is now televised in nearly every place people tend to gather, as background noise and wallpaper—at the corner sandwich shop where we grab lunch, at the restaurant bar where we meet friends after work, at the airport when we wait for our flight. It's as if we're being hypnotized. Add to that Internet blogs, radio talk show "shock jocks," and so-called reality TV in which people are encouraged to behave badly for our entertainment and is it any wonder we're a nation in depression?

The truth is, this hyper bad-news environment isn't giving us an accurate picture of our world. If we were aware of all the ways we humans—as individuals and in small groups and large organizations—spend our days being productive and creative, behaving with integrity and generosity and even courage, we would see that the good news outweighs the bad. If this wasn't so, we'd probably have annihilated ourselves by now.

Of course, it wouldn't make sense to go through life ignoring bad news. But to be a truly informed citizenry with a realistic view of the world, we need to see the whole picture, the triumphs as well as the challenges. A smaller and more balanced intake of news would make us all healthier.

Today, physicists, physicians, psychologists, in fact experts in nearly every field tell us—and there is plenty of research bearing this out—that we are physically and emotionally healthier when our beliefs and thoughts are positive and when we feel that our thoughts and actions matter. Some scientists, some quantum physicists in particular, go so far as to say that what we think literally creates the reality we experience.

The general consensus is this: The world around us is a reflection of what we think and believe. If we feel positive and generous, we act accordingly and attract people, circumstances, and events that reflect those qualities. If we're negative and fearful, the same applies. If this is true for us as individuals, the theory would also apply to groups, even to nations and the world, wouldn't it? In other words, a society that believes and focuses overwhelmingly on bad news will act accordingly and attract more of the same.

■   ■   ■

The most popular course at Harvard these days is Positive Psychology. When 855 students enrolled in spring 2006, it beat out even Introductory Economics. This is Harvard, an intelligent, serious, type-A bunch, so a "fluffy" psychology class beating out Intro Econ, that means something. The enrollment, as the students themselves commented in interviews, indicates a deep hunger for a more positive outlook.

Positive Psychology is based largely on the work of Martin Seligman, professor of psychology at the University of Pennsylvania and former president of the American Psychological Association. His work is supported by the National Institute of Mental Health, the National Institute of Aging, the National Science Foundation, and the Department of Education, among others, and has spawned a whole field of research. In short, the psychology world takes Seligman and Positive Psychology very seriously.

In the way the news industry does today, psychologists once focused almost exclusively on the negative—human suffering and mental problems. "We have studied abuse and anxiety, depression and disease, prejudice and poverty," explains David Myers, professor of psychology at Hope College. In fact, "articles on selected negative emotions since 1887 have outnumbered those on positive emotions 17 by 1" (*Psychology*, Worth, 8th edition, 2007). This focus told us very little about the workings of a mentally healthy person living a productive and contented life. But then, in the late '60s and early '70s, Seligman and others began to research how thinking and believing, among other things, affect our experience. Here are a few of Positive Psychology's findings:

- Optimism can protect people from mental and physical illness.

- Physicians experiencing positive emotion tend to make more accurate diagnoses.

- People who express gratitude on a regular basis have better physical health, optimism, progress toward goals, well-being, and help others more.

- People who witness others perform good deeds experience an emotion called "elevation," and this motivates them to perform their own good deeds.

- People who are optimistic or happy have better performance in work, school, and sports, are less depressed, have fewer physical health problems, and have better relationships with other people.

From my experience in researching and writing this book, I can report that regular doses of positive news contribute to an overall feeling of optimism. (It's amazing, really, how much my outlook has improved.) And, in addition to the benefits that this attitude brings mentally and physically, good news has another important side-effect: We learn from other people's actions and ideas. Great artists do this all the time; they borrow and merge ideas from an array of sources to create something new and their own. Dickens was inspired and influenced by the works of Jane Austen; James Joyce was inspired and influenced by the works of Dickens, and so on. We do this in our own work. A colleague comes up with a clever solution to a tough problem, does a good deed or courageous act, and we're inspired to think and act in new ways. If we learn that FedEx has begun using hybrid trucks in their fleet (which they have), for example, and we hear about what the stumbling blocks and triumphs have been, it might spark us to translate the idea to our own company. Positive news nourishes our hearts and minds, educates and informs us, and inspires us to take action.

There are many journalists and news outlets we can admire for their integrity and sound reporting, so this book is not a screed against The Media. It's more of a call for all of us, news industry and news consumers, to become more aware of what we're calling news, how much we're consuming, and how it's affecting us individually and collectively. Because the bottom line is, there's plenty of encouraging news out there once we switch our focus to it. There are people everywhere, everyday—individuals as well as governments and even Big Corporations—who are making the world a better place. And they remind us that the beliefs, thoughts, and actions of the individual DO make a difference.

■   ■   ■

To find the good news stories you're about to read, I scoured regional, national, and international news sources—print, TV, radio, and Internet—as well as independent and governmental organizations. Throughout the book, I also share some of the best resources I've found, those that have informed and inspired me and that I refer to again and again.

I want you to know I have no personal or business relationship with any of the individuals, companies, or organizations included in this book. (I have an indirect relationship with St. Francis House, featured on page 53, only in that my husband works for the Clarks Companies North America and Clarks is a St. Francis House sponsor.) I've received no compensation of any kind from any person or group you're about to meet. I have included them for no other reason than that I believe you'll benefit from knowing them.

So now—on to the good news!

For a more extensive list of Positive Psychology findings, history of the field, and practical resources, visit Martin Seligman and the Positive Psychology Center at the University of Pennsylvania: www.ppc.sas.upenn.edu.

Two books I highly recommend: *Learned Optimism* by Martin P. Seligman, Ph.D. (Vintage, 2006 edition) presents, as the Philadelphia *Daily News* says, "a system for reforming the most entrenched pessimist." It also includes the fascinating history of Positive Psychology.

Mindset: The New Psychology of Success by psychologist Carol S. Dweck, Ph.D. (Random House, 2006) will help you understand your particular style of thinking and how it might be holding you back. This book will also help you deal more effectively with the children in your life. Dweck's research has shown that the blanket praise we give children is often not in their best interest. She offers new ways to encourage and empower our kids and ourselves.

The Headlines

Positive News and Trends

char-i-ty

noun / benevolent goodwill toward or love of humanity • voluntary
generosity and helpfulness especially toward the needy or
suffering • aid given to those in need • an institution, organization,
or fund established to aid those in need • public provision for the
relief of the needy • lenient judgment of others • mercy

for-give-ness

noun / the act of forgiving • the excusing of a fault or an offense
• pardoning • the giving up of anger or resentment against
someone

It's a beautiful word, *charity*. Love, goodwill, generosity,
mercy—that's what I found repeatedly in my good news search.
What you'll find in the following stories are individuals and
organizations giving their time, attention, money, and even forgiveness, often to complete strangers.

While compiling this section, I was reminded of the beautiful lines from Indian poet Tagore's *Stray Birds*: "Once we

dreamt that we were strangers. We wake up to find that we were dear to each other."

Charity by the Numbers

Charitable giving continues to rise and volunteering has reached a 30-year high. That's good news enough, but what's most exciting is the growing trend—young corporate leaders sharing their wealth now, instead of waiting until they're gone, launching philanthropic foundations the likes of which we've never seen; TV, movie, sport, and music stars using their celebrity status to call attention to causes that we haven't focused on in the past; "average" individuals giving their time and money to help perfect strangers in the wake of 9/11 and Hurricane Katrina.

There is a new standard being set and it's bringing us to a new awareness, inspiring us to give more and get involved. Here are some impressive numbers:

$260.3 billion—the amount Americans donated to charity in 2005, an almost $15 billion increase over 2004, according to the American Association of Fundraising Counsel's yearbook of philanthropy, *Giving USA*. (Donation tally for 2006 should be released in June 2007, after this book has gone to press. Check with givingusa.org to see how we did.)

76.5%—the portion of the $260.3 billion that was donated by individual living donors. Like you and me. According to *Giving USA*, individuals are always the largest single source of donations. Meaning our contributions really do add up. The rest comes from foundations, corporations, and the bequests of deceased individuals.

70–80%—the percentage of Americans who contribute annually to at least one charity. The American Association of Fundraising Counsel reports, "Living individuals account for three-quarters of total charitable giving in the U.S. and have done so since *Giving USA* began publication [in 1956]. . . . Being a 'philanthropist' does not merely mean making huge gifts; it means giving to any cause that you value."

65.4 million—the number of Americans who donated their time—on average 50 hours—to charities in 2005, a 30-year high. (A hard number to beat, considering the surge of volunteers in the aftermath of Hurricane Katrina; preliminary 2006 figures indicate there's been a slight drop, so let's get going.)

16–19—the age group that more than doubled its volunteering rates from 1989 to 2005. "We are encouraged that emerging studies consistently show increased volunteering by young Americans," said Robert T. Grimm, Jr., Director of

Research and Policy Development at the Corporation for National and Community Service. "If supported properly, we may be on the cusp of a new civic generation."

33.2%—the rate of volunteering for Baby Boomers; they have the highest rate of volunteering of all age groups. Far from being the "Me Generation," they are volunteering at sharply higher rates than did the previous generation at mid-life. They volunteer an average of 51 hours per year.

64%—the increase from 1974 to 2005 among Americans aged 65 and over who volunteer.

5—the top ranking states for overall, all-ages volunteering: Utah, Nebraska, Minnesota, Iowa, Alaska. To see where your state ranks in volunteering, go to nationalservice.gov/about/volunteering/index.asp.

15%—the increase in volunteers the Corporation for National and Community Service hopes to see over the next five years. Why not help them reach their goal? Go ahead and volunteer at that program you've been thinking about.

Living in a State of Generosity

Way to go Utah, Oklahoma, Nebraska, Minnesota, and Georgia! You are the five most generous states in the na-

Want to volunteer but not sure where to start? There are plenty of reputable organizations who will get you moving in the right direction. Here are just a few good places to start your search: Idealist.org, United Way (unitedway.org), and VolunteerMatch.org. For in-depth information and inspiration regarding both charitable giving and volunteering, visit *The Chronicle of Philanthropy* (philanthropy.com) and the American Association of Fundraising Counsel's yearbook of philanthropy, *Giving USA* (givingusa.org).

tion, according to a new report by the NewTithing Group, "Wealth & Generosity by State." (Are *you* living in a state of generosity? Go to newtithing.com. You may be surprised.)

The NewTithing report reveals that generous states actually ranked low in wealth. In fact, the report calculates that if affluent income-tax filers in just the five wealthiest states— California, New York, Florida, Texas, and Illinois—gave as generously as do their less affluent peers in those Most Charitable Five states, individual giving in the U.S. would increase $13 billion a year.

And thus the challenge is set. May the most generous state win!

Focus-Worthy Resource

Before You Write That Generous Check

Where do you want to put your energy? If you believe, as I do, that everything has energy, including thoughts, beliefs, and money, it makes sense to donate to an organizations that supports causes for which you have a personal interest or, better yet, a passion. What resonates with you? Making sure children have enough to eat? Education for adults with disabilities? The environment? Animal welfare?

Once you've decided what kind of charity should receive your energy, take a little time to figure out which organization will make your money work hardest. After all, what good is your $10, $100, or $1 million if the organization handling it is so inefficient your money is only going to pay salaries or fundraising expenses?

Just how *do* we know which charities are the most efficient and worth donating to?

Charity Navigator to the rescue. It's on *Time* magazine's "50 Coolest Websites" list and Forbes' "Best of the Web," too. Deservedly. This well-organized site offers practical and just plain interesting information. What *are* the 10 biggest charities? Which charities are routinely in the red? Which are the most efficient? How do the biggest celebrity-endorsed charities perform? Visit charitynavigator.org and find out.

Based on the annual tax forms each charity provides, Charity Navigator evaluates two areas of financial health—organizational efficiency and "capacity," meaning how well a charity can sustain its efforts over time—and issues a zero- to four-star rating. The ratings indicate how effectively a charity will use your money today, how it will grow its programs and services over time, and how it compares to its peers.

Remember, though, that while these ratings provide a valuable indicator, we need to consider all factors when deciding on a charity. One of my favorites, for example, received a low Charity Navigator score. So I did a little checking and discovered that the organization had recently undergone a major expansion. The charity was still doing good work, and efficiently, but their debt ratio was high, a red flag, hence their low rating. With just a little effort, I had enough information to feel confident in making a donation.

A nonprofit organization itself, Charity Navigator was founded in 2001 and funded by New York philanthropists John and Marion Dugan who believed "an unbiased charity evaluator needed to be created to help benevolent citizens make informed giving decisions." Charity Navigator doesn't charge users to access its rating information. (Donate to Charity Navigator? What a great idea.)

Set aside an evening and explore. Read the FAQs section from start to finish. You'll be a smarter donor for it. And the

Giving Calculator is a fun way to help you determine how much you can afford to donate annually. (Have you ever actually planned how much you'll give in the year ahead?) The Tips section is invaluable, with topics such as what to do when a charity calls, tax issues, advice for older donors, and giving in times of crisis; there's even a guide to giving in the workplace. Charity Navigator's president, Trent Stamp, also writes a blog that's informative and just a tad snarky. (Doting pet owners—you know who you are—read "My Holiday Idea to Save the World.")

Meanwhile, courtesy of Charity Navigator, here's a tip everyone should keep in mind when those telemarketers call, in the middle of dinner:

Hang Up the Phone / Eliminate the Middleman

Informed donors recognize that for-profit fundraisers, those primarily used in charitable telemarketing campaigns, keep 25 to 95 cents of every dollar they collect. Informed donors never give out their personal information—like credit card accounts, social security numbers—over the phone. If they like what they hear in the pitch, they'll hang up, investigate the charity online, and send their contribution directly to the charity, thereby cutting out the middleman and ensuring 100 percent of their donation reaches the charity.

Women's Group Discovers
Giving Never Tasted So Good

In 2002, Marsha Wallace of Greenville, South Carolina, read an article about a group of social workers who got together for potluck dinners and, with the money they would have spent in restaurants, made donations to needy families. Inspired by the story, Wallace started *Dining for Women* with 20 women meeting for a potluck dinner and raising $750. Since then, the organization has achieved a tax exempt status and has 47 chapters in over 23 states and in Italy and Australia.

In 2006 alone, DFW gave over $50,000 to charitable organizations chosen by the group. "Our focus is exclusively on international women's and/or children's programs and the education of our members is critical to our mission," Wallace says. "Our model is based on three things: learning, dining, and giving. We offer educational programs for the charities that we contribute to each month so our members can learn about the specific cultural issues facing women we are trying to help, and to foster connections between our members and the program recipients."

All DFW chapters contribute to the same program each month, so the impact is much greater than if they gave individually. By spring of 2007, the monthly gifts were averaging between $5,000 and $6,000.

DFW is starting to get some media attention, Wallace says. Won't it be fun to see how many new chapters spring up as a result?

Visit *Dining for Women*'s friendly and informative site, diningforwomen.org, for information about how to start your own group—or just to spark your imagination to create your own personalized charity project.

May 1 Suggest . . . Fun and Easy Ways to Develop Your Child's Anterior Prefrontal Cortex

(Hint: It's an area of the brain, evolved relatively recently and thought to be unique to humans. It's involved in complex decision making when self-interest and moral beliefs are in conflict.) Have your kids create a pennies-for-change bucket. Anything sturdy will do. A shoebox, a bowl, a coffee can. Let them get creative and decorate it, then put it in a place that will be handy to everybody in the family. On the table near the front door, on the kitchen counter, wherever you all pass or gather regularly. At the end of each day, drop in the change from your pockets or purses. Little kids love noise—start a healthy competition of whose daily donation makes the biggest clatter.

Every six months, take the change to your bank for counting—at most banks this is a free service—and have them deposit it into your checking account. Once it's deposited, gather together everyone who has contributed to the pot and ceremoniously write out a check to a charity you've all researched and decided upon. (For help deciding on a charity, refer to charitynavigator.org above or consider microlending; see page 44.)

Your kids develop big brains and big hearts.

One Woman's Determination Illustrates
That We Can Always Make a Difference

If you ever find yourself giving up on a cherished goal, the story of 88-year-old Maisie DeVore of Eskridge, Kansas, will keep you going.

Over 30 years ago, Maisie dreamed of a place where the kids of her small rural community could have some fun. So, she decided to start saving money to build a community swimming pool. She made and sold jams and jellies and afghans, held yard sales; she asked people she knew to collect cans, which she recycled. And each month for nearly three decades, she set out in her pickup truck to collect cans and scrap metals, car batteries, and junk from the roadsides around Wabaunsee County. She'd crush the cans, get the other junk ready, and haul her collection to a recycling center in Topeka.

Little by little, Maisie DeVore was able to save an amazing $73,000. With additional help from the state of Kansas and some private donations, the pool fund finally totaled $170,000 and in the summer of 2001, after a parade and opening ceremony, Maisie's dream came true—the kids of Eskridge and surrounding communities took their first swim in Maisie's Community Swimming Pool, which, appropriately enough, sits across the street from Maisie's home.

Since then, summer attendance at the pool averages about 100 people per day. The pool also serves Heritage Village, a challenged-adult community, as well as seniors, civic organizations, and citizens who find relief and treatment for medical ailments. It is, in the true sense of the word, a community pool.

To view a powerful two-minute mini-documentary, go to youtube.com and type "Maisie DeVore" into the search field. If watching and hearing Maisie tell her story doesn't give you a shot of Get Up and Go, nothing will.

The pool project continues—there are bills to pay, maintenance, sewer, and liability insurance. Her old pickup died, so she's driving an old car on her junk rounds these days; and a volunteer now helps her by taking the loads to Topeka, but she's still at it. (If you'd like to give Maisie and the kids of Eskridge a hand, visit maisiespool.com, or write to DeVore Community Swimming Pool Association, PO Box 233, Eskridge, KS 66423.)

She's had a lot of setbacks along the way, she says, but she keeps going. "If you think you can't do anything, you probably won't," Maisie says. "But, if you really have a project that you believe in, even if you're not up to what you were several years ago, you can still do a lot of things. If you want something and pursue it with all of your mind, you'll get it done one way or another."

One Man's Generosity and Forethought
Keep Him Alive for Posterity

When he died in 1948, Frank P. Doyle, a businessman and civic leader in Santa Rosa, California, had already contributed much to his community, but with his last will and testament, he gave a gift that keeps on giving, a lot.

As the cofounder and second president of the Exchange Bank, a community bank started by Doyle and his father in 1890, his will established a perpetual charitable trust in which he placed 51 percent of his bank stock. The dividends of the stock would fund the Frank P. Doyle and Polly O'Meara Doyle Scholarship Fund, to be distributed to Santa Rosa Junior College for individual scholarships. As a result, over 100,000 students have received a free education at one of the top community colleges in the United States.

Founded in 1918, Santa Rosa Junior College, with its 100-plus acres of rolling hills and ivy-covered halls, was modeled as a junior version of nearby University of California at Berkeley. It was intended to be, and remains, a school whose graduates often continue their education by going on to the U.C. system. It's a vital part of Sonoma County.

The funds for the scholarship have an interesting history, too, one tied securely to the community. In 1890, after working in gold mines, breeding horses, and founding a stage company, Manville Doyle negotiated with local businessmen to launch Exchange Bank. He and his son, Frank, posted the working capital and held control from the beginning. Frank was determined that the bank remain a locally owned and managed community institution. And it has. The bank's mission statement actually states that it will be "an independent conservatively run community bank forever."

Every year Exchange Bank cuts a check for Santa Rosa Junior College. In 2006, it amounted to approximately $5 million, providing around 5,500 scholarships. Bank CEO J. Barrie Graham says the bank has been profitable for 117 years, and the trust and its dividends have amounted to around $75 million for the scholarship.

Some Santa Rosa families have received a scholarship each generation. It's a beautiful legacy. Nearly 60 years after his death, Frank P. Doyle is still alive and contributing to his community.

Where Have All the Billionaires Gone?

It's been covered in the mainstream media, which is good news, but let's explore the Bill & Melinda Gates/Warren Buffet charity donation story from a slightly different angle. Because it's a potential paradigm-shifting development that's likely to benefit us all in a very positive way.

Bill Gates, cofounder of Microsoft and the world's wealthiest person, may have started something more world altering than even his dream of a PC on every desk. Along with wife Melinda Gates and friend Warren Buffett, he apparently dreams of a world where all people are fed, healthy, and educated.

In August 1999, Gates and his wife, Melinda, donated $6 billion to their Bill & Melinda Gates Foundation. It earned them a spot in the *Guinness Book of World Records* for the largest single private charitable donation ever made. They have since donated billions more, some reports saying as high as $24 billion. They were out-donated, however, when Warren Buffet, the world's second wealthiest person, pledged 85 percent of his Berkshire Hathaway fortune to the foundation, a value of $30.7 billion. The pledge, to be paid in specified payments over time, is, according to the *Chronicle of Philanthropy*, the largest charitable donation ever made.

They're known to be close friends, and although we can't confirm reports that Bill and Melinda actually get together with Warren for a competitive game of bridge, it's fun to imagine the conversation if they did.

"Ha, I won another hand!" crows Warren, sipping his Cherry Coke. "I'm feeling generous. How about I donate $30 billion to your foundation?"

"Oh, come on, Warren," says Bill, passing the mixed nuts. "You can do better than that."

"Make it at least $30.7 billion," says Melinda, munching a filbert, "or you'll just look cheap. Good nuts."

The result: The Gates Foundation is the largest grant-making foundation in the world, with these two stated values as its core:

- All lives—no matter where they are being led—have equal value.

- To whom much has been given, much is expected.

As stated on the official site, gatesfoundation.org, the foundation has three areas of focus:

- Global Development Program: aims to help hundreds of millions of families in the developing world emerge from extreme poverty and hunger.

- United States Program: works to ensure that America's most vulnerable people, particularly at-risk children and youth, have access to educational opportunities.

- Global Health Program: funds research to develop effective, affordable solutions to health issues common to developing countries.

As of September 2006, the Gates endowment is $31.9 billion (which includes $1.6 billion from the first installment of Buffett's gift), with grant commitments such as these:

- United Negro College Fund, Gates Millennium Scholars Program—$1 billion

- Malaria Vaccine Initiative—$258 million

- Save the Children, Saving Newborn Lives—$110 million

- United Way of King County, Seattle, WA—$55 million

- Knowledgeworks Foundation—$20 million

- National Council of Culture & Arts, Mexico Library Project—$11.7 million

- Public Access Computing Hardware Upgrade Program, Multiple Library Systems—$5.3 million

Of course, there are critics who don't agree with some of the specific organizations to which the foundation contributes.

Fair enough, we'll never all agree on where the money is best spent. But furthering education, improving health, reducing poverty—who can argue with that? And really, can anyone argue that this isn't a good thing, billionaires giving away billions for the ultimate benefit of all?

Both the Gateses and Buffett have made statements to the effect that they aren't in favor of transferring enormous fortunes from one generation to the next, which may be a trend. According to the Forbes 2006 "America's 400 Richest" list, 34 people from the 2005 list had dropped off because they either "couldn't keep up or gave their money away." Husband-and-wife banking team Herbert and Marion Sandler, for instance, dropped from Forbes rankings after giving away more than $1 billion to charity.

Now that would be something to see, wouldn't it, a Forbes Richest 400 with listees' wealth only in the millions. Where have all the billionaires gone, we'll ask. Why, they've given their money to charity, of course.

And just what will Bill Gates, the individual, specifically bring to the world of philanthropy? In November 2006, Gates discussed his thoughts on *The Charlie Rose Show*. Rose asked Gates why he chose to leave Microsoft to run the foundation full time when there was so much going on in technology and when he was so clearly excited just talking about it.

"It's unusual that I have another activity, which has been part time for me," Gates answered, referring to his role at the foundation, "that is so interesting that it is somewhat more compelling for me and perhaps, you know—I think there's more of a vacuum in terms of what I can bring to it . . ."

"Why is it more compelling?" Rose asked.

Because there are fewer models, Gates explained. "In the area of, say, global health, really assembling the scientists and giving them the right resources and cutting through the complex way that you do these drug trials and the complex issues about getting them delivered so they have a big impact, that is almost like when the microprocessor came along, where the opportunity is there, but you've got to put the pieces together in a different way than it's been done before."

Seeing the problem in a new way, putting the pieces together in a way that's never been done before—creating a new paradigm of charity and giving. If anyone has experience in

Visit CharlieRose.com to listen to Rose's full interview with Bill Gates. It's a thought-provoking discussion in which Rose and Gates consider the possible future of technology and philanthropy and also the current and potential role of the U.S. in world.

If you aren't already aware of it, many TV and radio broadcasts are available on the programs' Web sites, usually for free. Which means we can take control and listen to what we want, when and where we will.

creating a new paradigm, it's Bill Gates. How exciting to see what he creates this time.

Three News Stories Remind Us That to Err Is Human and to Forgive Is, Too

Stories of retaliation and eye-for-an-eye justice are commonplace in the mainstream news headlines. In my good news search, however, I've been surprised again and again by stories in which individuals and groups have demonstrated the human ability to forgive others, often for enormous transgressions. With each story I've encountered, it becomes more and more clear—the sincere bestowing of forgiveness is fundamental to our humanity.

The following three news items illustrate the power of forgiveness for both the giver and the receiver.

In 2003, the *Boston Globe* reported the story of Dennis Maher, who in 1983, at the age of 23, stepped into a nightmare. Maher was accused of committing three brutal rapes. Although he asserted his innocence and no biological evidence linked him to the crime, he was convicted and sentenced to life imprisonment.

To make the story of a very long and difficult struggle short: In 2003, at age 42, having served 19 years, two months, and 29 days, Maher was released from prison; new DNA evidence concluded that he could not have committed the crimes.

In an interview in the February 2007 issue of O magazine, Maher, now married with a young daughter, describes the day of his release.

> In the courtroom, my mom didn't recognize me. She hadn't seen me in a suit in 19 years. I was clean-shaven. I still had chains on my ankles and wrists, but I looked good. The guards took off the chains, and I hugged my parents and my lawyer. Then J.W. Carney, the man who had prosecuted me 19 years earlier, asked to speak to me. He said "I'm sorry, Dennis. I did not know." He said, "Can you forgive me?" I said, "I forgive you, Jay." He had the guts to step forward and apologize. And he still gets picked on for it. I was one of the first exonerees to get a face-to-face apology—which went a long way toward helping me get through this.

In 2006, the nation was horrified to hear of a school shooting in an Amish community in Pennsylvania. One deeply troubled man went into a one-room schoolhouse and shot 10 little girls, killing five and seriously injuring five others. He then shot himself.

What is most telling about all the reporting that surrounded the event, however, was not the shock over the shootings themselves, but the shock over the Amish community's response to the shootings. With a quiet dignity, the community spoke of forgiving the man responsible, Charles Carl Roberts IV. Roberts had "problems of the heart," they said, and they came together not only to comfort and aid each other, but, astonishingly, also to comfort and aid Roberts's family.

In an *ABC News* report (October 3, 2006), Charles Gibson reported that Amish midwife Rhita Rhoads, who was present for the births of two of the girls who were killed, said, simply enough, "If you have Jesus in your heart and he has forgiven you . . . [how] can you not forgive other people?"

Twenty-two years after one of the most horrendous cases of genocide in modern times, a traditional form of participatory justice is helping to heal ravaged Rwanda. In 1994, Rwanda's Hutu majority, organized and urged on by the government, attempted to "cleanse" the small nation of its Tutsi minority. Over 800,000 were murdered, mostly Tutsis, but also some Hutus who refused to support the genocide. Neighbors killing neighbors.

Today, a key figure in the story of Rwanda's journey toward healing is Aloisea Inyumba, formerly a minister with the government's Unity and Reconciliation Commission and now a senator in the Rwandan government. In "Forgiveness Is a

Journey" (*Ode*, October 2006) journalist and photographer Lekha Singh reports on the progress in Rwanda. With her kind permission, the following is excerpted from her article:

"After the genocide, we were faced by the enormous and almost impossible task of restoring unity in a community the very fabric of which had fallen apart," [Senator Aloisea Inyumba] explains. "No one wanted to talk about reconciliation. Even I had to question myself . . . am I genuine?"

But amnesty was out of the question. So Inyumba and other Rwandan leaders studied how truth and reconciliation commissions had worked in South Africa and Ireland to ease bloody conflicts. But she notes, "Here it was not about establishing the truth. Everyone knew what that was. The communities knew who had done what, and to whom."

Aware that imported reconciliation programs would not work for a human disaster of such magnitude, Inyumba also saw that Rwanda's court system, slow and backlogged was failing to administer justice. In 1999, five years after the massacres, only a few thousand of 120,000 accused murderers had been tried. So Inyumba and others conducted a national survey asking people three basic questions to find a way to begin a process of healing:

1. Do you think reconciliation is possible?

2. If yes, what do you think we should do?

3. Are you going to be a part of this process?

"We realized there could be no reconciliation without the full engagement of the community," she says. "So we went back to the traditional Rwandan form of resolving conflict, the Gacaca (pronounced ga-CHA-cha) process, and modified it. Classic justice could not work here, so we opted for participatory justice."

Gacaca is a "hands-on" system in which the victim and the accused meet at the scene of the brutality and talk about what happened in the presence of the community. The accused confesses to what he or she did. The witnesses from the community present their versions of the truth. In these cases, it is generally easy to identify what happened, since the violence was done in public. The victims are allowed to open up, share and cry, but they cannot take revenge. Citizens are selected by the community and agree to serve in the process as counselors call *Inyangamugayo*, or "people of integrity." They wear an identifying green sash during the proceedings.

The leaders of the genocide, those in authority, notorious murderers and those guilty of rape and sexual torture remain in prison and are tried in their communities, with one of more than 250,000 Inyangamugayo presiding and each proceeding attended by some 90 percent of the community members.

At the two sessions I witnessed in Kigali, there were no demonstrations of anger, even with the very hard questions asked by the family of the victims, the Inyangamugayo, and the community. One involved the murder of a woman and two children. The other concerned property damage.

A government release assessing the Gacaca process found a number of benefits:

- It discloses the truth about what happened during the genocide and establishes individual responsibility.
- It reduces suspicion among Rwandans and dispels rumors and distrust.
- It does not require money.
- It accelerates the trial process, ending the wait for both victims and perpetrators as well as transforming the culture of impunity that existed when no justice had been done.
- It facilitates prosecution since the Inyangamugayo are charged with community service.
- The penalties imposed by the Gacaca courts are designed to integrate the guilty person into society and

enable him to participate with others in the recon-
struction of the country, instead of further derailing
it with the expenses involved in detaining hundreds
of thousands of people in prison.

I ask Senator Inyumba if there is real forgiveness
between the Hutu and Tutsi. "Forgiveness is a journey," she says. "At the end of the journey we come to
the conclusion that we are more similar than different,
with common problems and concerns. It is in the interest of both groups to build the road and to live and
work together. Our mission cannot be conflict."

One of the biggest signs of forgiveness has been the
foster parenting of something approaching 400,000
orphaned children. Widows, ministers and Hutu and
Tutsi alike have taken these children into their homes.
It is not unusual to hear a Hutu woman say she has six
children of which four are Tutsi orphans. One female
minister of state has adopted 18 children.

Focus-Worthy Resource

A Magazine for Intelligent Optimists

One of my favorite alternative news sources
is *Ode* magazine. In 10 issues a year, *Ode* cov-

ers newsworthy events from around the world that tend to get missed by mainstream news sources, news stories such as Lekha Singh's "Forgiveness is a Journey," excerpted above.

Foreign Policy magazine had this to say about *Ode* in their March/April 2007 issue:

With [its] "we are the world" perspective, it would be easy to dismiss *Ode* as hyper-lefty, antiglobalization hokum. . . . But that oversimplication misses *Ode's* real potential as a laboratory for new ideas and solutions to the problems we'll face in the future. The [September 2006] cover story by Senior Editor Marco Visscher, for example, examined ways that innovative video games are improving education and learning retention in schools. A short article by Senior Editor Tijn Touber offered a balanced refutation of the myths of wind power. It's refreshing to read such articles that eschew scare tactics and hyperbole.

As an added bonus, *Ode* is nicely designed, often features beautiful photo spreads, and is printed on recycled paper. It's great reading for teenagers, too. So go ahead, give it a try for a year. To subscribe, call 888-633-6242 (that's a toll-free number) or go to odemagazine.com.

Spread the word, too. Next time you're stumped for a gift idea, give an *Ode* subscription. Your loved ones will receive a regular dose of good news and thank you for it.

Not to mention your conversations may take on a positive new twist.

in–vest

transitive verb / furnish with power or authority • grant someone control or authority over, vest • cover completely, envelop • clothe, adorn • endow with a quality • infuse • spend or devote for future benefit

em–power

transitive verb / to invest with power • give official authority or legal power • enable • promote the self-actualization or influence of • make someone stronger and more confident, especially in controlling their life and claiming their rights

---

Intelligence, drive, and creativity, these are words we often associate with the most privileged of our society. But what my good news search confirms is that these terms often apply to our most underprivileged as well, especially when they're given access to resources most of us take for granted—education, capital, and encouragement.

There's an amazing trend afoot. Empowered people—from business icons to celebrities to individuals like you and me—are investing in society by contributing to those we've so often overlooked. As the following stories illustrate, a little opportunity goes a long way.

Imagining a Museum of Poverty

It's a familiar story. An idea is ridiculed. Thirty years later, it wins prizes. A few years later still, it's just so *obvious*.

During the 1974 famine in Bangladesh, young economics professor Muhammad Yunus, a Fulbright scholar and graduate of Vanderbilt University, was teaching at Chittagong University, in Bangladesh. "I found myself in a very strange situation," Yunus says. "Teaching elegant theories of economics, telling all my students that every economic problem has beautiful solutions. And I walk out of the classroom, those elegant theories have no use for people who were dying" ("Banking on People," *NewsHour*, April 24, 2001).

So, he talked to the poor and experimented with ways of helping them. He loaned $27 to a group of Bangladeshi women so they could buy bamboo to make and sell furniture in their village. They had no collateral, and he didn't ask them to pay back the money. But they did. And seeing the results, Yunus was convinced that he had a solution to their problem: microcredit.

Microcredit—or microlending or microfinancing, depending on who's doing the talking—is generally defined as small lending to the rural poor. "To solve the problem of poverty, you have to start thinking differently," Yunus says. His theory is that you have to put people in a position where they can use their own skills and initiative to build their own lives. "Lend the poor money in amounts which suit them, teach them a few sound financial principles, and they manage on their own" (2006 Nobel Prize presentation speech).

Here are the facts:

- Grameen Bank (Grameen meaning "village" or "rural" in Bangladeshi) began informally in 1976 and formally in 1983. It is the world's largest bank for the poor. Through their deposits, poor people own 90% of the bank; the remaining 10% is owned by the government of Bangladesh. The bank is self-financing and makes a profit.

- Since its formal opening in 1983, Grameen Bank has loaned almost $6 billion: $800 million per year, in loans averaging just over $100. It has over seven million borrowers.

- Poor people organize themselves into groups, often five women. The group is granted the loan—no collateral required—and is responsible for repayment.

Group members meet regularly to support and educate one another and also network with other groups.

- Over 95% of the borrowers are women. Third-world banks have traditionally only loaned money to men. What Yunus found, however, was that the women of Bangladesh do far better with the money loaned. Men tend to want to spend the money right away, for enjoyment and entertainment, while the women look at it as something to help their children and families in the long term.

- The loan payback rate is estimated at 98%.

- There are now microcredit programs in nearly 100 countries all over the world.

While microcredit was ridiculed at the beginning, the United Nations designated 2005 as the International Year of Microcredit, and in 2006, Muhammad Yunus won the Nobel Peace Prize. "Yunus's long-term vision is to eliminate poverty in the world," the Norwegian Nobel Committee said of Yunus and his work. "That vision cannot be realized by means of microcredit alone. But Muhammad Yunus and Grameen Bank have shown that in the continuing efforts to achieve it, micro-credit must play a major part."

At the prize presentation in Oslo, Norway, on December 10, 2006, Professor Ole Danbolt Mjøs, chairman of the Norwegian Nobel Committee, said, "By means of this year's Peace Prize award, the Norwegian Nobel Committee wishes to focus attention on dialogue with the Muslim world, on the women's perspective, and on the fight against poverty. . . . Muhammad Yunus has shown himself to be a leader who has managed to turn visions into practical action for the benefit of millions of people, not only in Bangladesh but also in many other countries."

Shortly before he won his Nobel Peace Prize, *Time* magazine asked Yunus, "You said a decade ago that our grandchildren will have to go to museums to see poverty. Do you still think that?"

"Absolutely," he replied. "Fifty-eight percent of the poor who borrowed from Grameen are now out of poverty. There are over 100 million people now involved with microcredit schemes. At the rate we're heading, we'll halve total poverty by 2015. We'll create a poverty museum in 2030" ("Q & A: Muhammad Yunus," *Time*, October 23, 2006).

"Museum of poverty! It's ridiculous!" says one critic. "To claim that microfinance is going to solve poverty is a myth. From ancient Greece to today, poverty has been with us and it will occupy us forever" (quoted in "Millions for Millions," *The New Yorker*, October 30, 2006).

It has been, therefore it shall always be. Yes, an excellent argument. Yet, we stand before the display case of powdered

In 2005, Muhammad Yunus had a chance meeting with Groupe Danone (that's Dannon yogurt) chairman and CEO, Franck Riboud, and suggested he open a company in Bangladesh, one that would produce fortified yogurt for children who suffer from malnutrition. Riboud did.

"We are currently working on some refinements," Yunus told *Worth* magazine (March 2007). "The yogurt cups are biodegradable, made of cornstarch, but I would like them to also be edible. There is a small amount of plastic in the material now that keeps the cups from being edible, but they are researching the technology."

Now that's one for the *If We Can Imagine It We Can Achieve It* file.

wigs or slave shackles or whalebone corsets, thinking, Can you *imagine*, we once thought that was *normal*. Something is a part of our everyday psyche—"it's just the way it is," we say—and then one day it winds up in a museum. Where it belongs.

Microcredit isn't a complete answer, but it is having a big, positive impact, perhaps most importantly and simply, on our thinking.

Focus-Worthy Resources

Becoming a Microlender,
It's Easier Than Online Dating

Now that you know what microcredit and micro-lending are, here are two organizations that will help you get involved. Both are reputable, one makes loans internationally, the other within the U.S.

- Loans made within the United States: ACCION USA, based in Boston, at accionusa.org.

- Loans made internationally: Kiva (a Swahili word meaning "agreement" or "unity") is based in California, at kiva.org.

The idea for both organizations is brilliantly simple. Small-business owners who otherwise wouldn't be able to get a loan in a traditional bank apply for a loan amount for a particular goal within their business. The loans range from about $75 to $2,000 for international loans and $500 to $25,000 in the U.S.

So, for example, log on to kiva.org, click on "lend," and begin browsing the profiles of the entrepreneurs applying for loans. (The process has been compared to online dating.) You, the lender, pick the business you'd like to support and, in increments of $25, lend a portion or the whole amount of the loan.

You make a credit card or PayPal payment to Kiva, who transfers the funds to their microcredit organization partner in the loan recipient's village or town. The partner's representative delivers the loan to the business owner. The business owner repays the loan (usually within six to 12 months), the money is returned to Kiva, and then to you. You can withdraw your money or re-loan it, again and again, as you wish.

So far, Kiva reports a 100 percent repayment rate on all businesses with completed loan terms. Nevertheless, they remind us that we're are making a *loan* and, therefore, taking a risk. They suggest that we split up our intended loan funds among several business owners to avoid the all-your-eggs-in-one-basket dilemma.

The whole process is fun and empowering for the lender as well as for the lendee. It could be another way to get your kids involved in giving. Let them browse and make their own decisions—how much of their money to invest, to whom, and whether or not to reinvest when their loan is repaid.

I'll just bet they choose to reinvest.

In a New International Tournament, the Homeless Team Triumphs

In September 2006 in Cape Town, South Africa, hundreds packed a temporary stadium in front of city hall. Even President Mbeki and Archbishop Tutu are reported to have been there. The event: the Homeless World Cup, an annual soccer competition involving homeless men and women from 48 countries.

After the Russian team beat newcomers Kazakhstan by one goal, Mel Young, president and co-founder (with Harald Schmied) of the competition, praised the players for their spirit: "Congratulations to Russia, winners of the fourth Homeless World Cup in Cape Town. Each and every player here stands proud, stands triumphant. You have represented your country with honor. You are all fantastic. Congratulations on a great tournament."

Kazakhstan's team captain, Kalikov Yergali, displayed gracious sportsmanship, saying, in broken English, "Russia are our brothers. Many thanks to sport that unites classes and people."

Each player received a medal for participating and special trophies were awarded to the following players and teams:

- Slovakia, Best Fair Play Team
- Paraguay, Best Mixed Team
- Lindsay Cooper of Scotland, Best Female Player
- Ronald Siame of Zambia, Best Male Player
- Kazakhstan, Best Newcomer
- Elliott Clow of Canada, Best Goalkeeper

Since its beginning in 2003, the event has been sponsored by Nike and the UEFA (Union of European Football Associations) and has been a huge success—in Austria in 2003, Sweden in 2004, and Edinburgh in 2005. The games have even been endorsed by the United Nations.

Adolf Ogi, special adviser to the United Nations secretary-general on Sport for Development and Peace, sent his congratulations to the 2006 organizers, stating that the event is an "outstanding example of how the positive potential of sport can play a vital role in promoting health, education, development, and peace."

Ogi went on to point out, "Like many other events, projects and initiatives, which take place all over the world without being noticed by the broad public, the Homeless World Cup uses sport as an innovative instrument to build bridges between people, to overcome cultural differences, and to spread an atmosphere of tolerance."

Denmark will play host to the next tournament, in Copenhagen, July 2007. Eva Kjer Hansen, the Danish social minister and minister of women's rights, is looking forward to the event.

"I'm convinced," says Hansen, "that sports can improve the self-esteem and life quality of homeless and other socially marginalized people. Sport is an efficient way of creating and developing social communities." She added that the tournament demonstrates to the world "that socially marginalized groups are able and want to take responsibility for their lives."

Indeed, for the players the tournament has a very practical impact. According to the Homeless World Cup organization, over 77 percent of the players involved change their lives forever. They move on to find regular employment, come off drugs and alcohol, pursue education, improve their housing, and even play for semi-professional and professional football clubs.

For the 2007 games, a street soccer stadium will be erected in front of Copenhagen's city hall. "I hope that we can help to break down prejudices," says Mayor Mikkel Warming, "while also giving both players in the field and the audience some fun."

Visit homelessworldcup.org, where you can view a photo gallery, watch videos of the games, and join the fan club, too.

Put Your Guests to Work, They'll Thank You for It

St. Francis House, a nonprofit, non-sectarian comprehensive shelter for men and women 18 and over located in the heart of Boston, is the largest homeless shelter in New England. It serves more than 800 people every day of the year. To put that in perspective, within a three month period in 2006, they served 74,213 meals, filled 1,983 clothing requests, provided

1,672 showers and 2,185 medical appointments, and counseled 5,014 guests at general and psychiatric counseling sessions.

Grounded in the spirit of St. Francis of Assisi, the staff and volunteers sincerely work to provide the poor and homeless a safe, respectful, and dignified refuge, and a sense of community. But what's so impressive about St. Francis House, even beyond the fact that they serve so many and with such care, is the breadth of services they offer the men and women who walk through the door. What began as a simple breadline in 1984 has grown into a multi-service source of hope for many.

In addition to all the basic services provided, St. Francis House offers job skills training and transitional housing. Three floors of the shelter's 11 stories, for example, are dedicated to the Next Step Housing Program, which provides an affordable, independent living situation and supportive community for men and women who've struggled with chronic homelessness, unemployment, and substance abuse.

One of the most successful programs at St. Francis House is the Moving Ahead Program (MAP). Once guests have their basic needs met—men and women who come to the shelter for help are referred to as guests, a simple yet meaningful gesture—they have the opportunity to apply to become MAP students. Developed by St. Francis House, MAP is a 14-week job- and life-skills training program that focuses on education, self-improvement, and creating long-term goals.

"Have you ever been asked to describe yourself?" asks Karen LaFrazia, St. Francis House executive director. "If you're like most of us, you list your occupation right up there with words about personality and the color of your hair. A job is important because it enables us to be self-sufficient. It feeds our souls as well. It's a sign that we are making a contribution, that we matter. Without that validation, it's all too easy to slip into depression that can be hard to escape."

Employment at St. Francis House, then, is viewed not as an end goal but as an essential part of the life-rebuilding process. MAP helps students prepare physically and mentally to find and retain jobs geared to their individual talents and skills. Students explore possible careers, learn about employer expectations, and set goals. (The program is explained in detail at stfrancishouse.org.)

Before heading to their chosen internships, students are off to "Studio Shine." The creation of Rose Harmon, a St. Francis House alum herself, the boutique is staffed by an image consultant specializing in working with the homeless. Students receive a consult and go through a first-impressions workshop. And since looking marvelous goes a long way to making us feel marvelous—and confident and ready to face the world—each student receives a week's worth of business attire, up-to-date and tailored to suit them.

Clarks Companies North America (Clarks shoes) is a sponsoring business and today one of its most valued employees is

Gregory Smith, a St. Francis House alum. Leah Bloom, development communications associate at St. Francis House, tells his story:

When the time came to apply for an internship, Gregory applied to be one of the four MAP students who would inaugurate the Clarks workplace immersion program, and was accepted. From his first day on the job, the internship was like nothing he'd ever experienced. "I could see the love," he says. "Everyone was like one big family." From the shoe designers to the marketing team to the human resources staff, everyone, including the president of the company made time for Gregory and his fellow interns. In awe to this day, Gregory says, "It blew me away."

Three days a week for four weeks, Gregory and his classmates rode the train together then took a cab to the Clarks corporate office. They had their own cubicles and computers, and began each morning by checking their email for the day's schedule. After rotating through the divisions of the company, they spent the last day of their internship at the flagship Clarks store, shadowing the sales team on the floor.

Gregory was fascinated. "I didn't want my internship to stop there," he says. He knew he wanted to pursue sales, so he extended his internship another week, during which he stayed in the store watching how the Clarks team sold shoes. His manager was so impressed that he stopped to talk with Gregory, who told him he was looking for a job. The manager had him fill out an application, and Gregory was hired right away.

"I've been there ever since," says Gregory. He's been clean and sober for over two years, and working at Clarks for over a year.

"I get up in the morning, get on my knees, and thank God for waking me up," he says. Then, "I jump on the [subway], get to my job, and start working." He's an expert on the products, his customers love him, and the nine-plus hour days fly by. Gregory is now on Clarks' management track. He even hopes to own his own shoe store someday.

It's the small, daily challenges that can trip us up, and an important facet of the MAP program is the support students and graduates receive not only while they're at their internships, but ongoing. Similar to a college or university, St. Francis House provides an Alumni Center with access to staff members and resources. There are also ongoing alumni events for socializing and support.

To date, over 700 men and women have graduated from the MAP program and there's a waiting list of nearly 300.

Replicas of the program are also being used in shelters in Topeka, Kansas, and St. Louis, Missouri.

Similar to microlending, the Moving Ahead Program is based on a formula that's really quite simple: respect people's humanity, give them resources, support, and responsibility, and allow them to empower themselves.

As Gregory puts it, "What I'm looking for is to be happy . . . be a responsible person, take care of my family, be a productive member of society. That's all I want."

More Colleges and Universities Are
Giving Students the Break They Really Need

A major development at America's institutions of higher learning: From Ivy-League schools like Princeton, Harvard, Stanford, and Yale to state institutions like the University of Virginia, Michigan State, Miami University in Ohio, University of Pennsylvania, and Rice University, a growing number of colleges and universities are offering free and/or greatly reduced tuition for accepted students from low- and middle-income families.

The tuition programs vary from school to school. Princeton's admissions page states: "the university admits undergraduate students without regard to their family financial circumstances and provides 100 percent of determined need. Since the 2001–02 academic year, no Princeton aid student, domestic of international, has been required to take out a loan to pay for his or her education" (see princeton.edu). At Harvard, accepted students in families with incomes of less than $40,000 will no longer be expected to contribute to the cost of tuition; and for families with incomes between $40,000 and $60,000, the contribution they're expected to make has been reduced (harvard.edu).

Some smaller and/or specialized schools are doing even better. Olin College of Engineering, Curtis Institute of Music, Berea College, and CUNY Honors College, among others, offer full tuition scholarships to anyone who gets accepted, regardless of economic status. In most cases, students (and/or parents) are still responsible for housing, books, and other expenses, but when you consider that yearly tuition at these run over $30,000 a year, tuition scholarships could add up to savings of over $120,000 for many students and their families. Not having huge student loans to pay upon graduating is a dream come true for many.

Some state and community colleges, recognizing the importance of a local, high-quality workforce, are also offering tuition waivers and reductions, attracting students who might otherwise not even have considered the possibility of attending college.

Paying the tuition bill has never been much fun for anyone, but it may be getting a little easier for those who could use the break the most.

American Business Men and Women
Are Taking Charge of Their Destiny

"We are in the midst of the largest entrepreneurial surge this country has ever seen," reports *Fortune Small Business* magazine ("Everyone Wants To Start a Business," February 2007). "According to Small Business Administration projections, nearly 672,000 new companies with employees were created in 2005. This is the biggest business birthrate in U.S. history; 30,000 more startups than in 2004. . . . And the trend shows no signs of abating."

Good news, considering the Office of Advocacy, the small-business watchdog of the U.S. Small Business Administration, says small-business births are the most important factor propelling growth in gross state product, state personal income, and total state employment.

According to a September 2006 report from the Office of Advocacy:

- There are over 25 million small businesses in the U.S.

- Small-businesses drive the U.S. economy; they represent 99.7% of all businesses and employ 57.4 million people (or 50.6%) of the non-farm private sector workforce.

- Small-business owners tend to be more "clean and green." They live, work, and play where their busi-

nesses are located and know their families, neighbors, and employees will hold them accountable.

There's even more good news for women. According to
Margaret Heffernan, author of the inspiring and informative
book *How She Does It: How Women Entrepreneurs Are
Changing the Rules of Business Success* (Viking, 2007):

- 40% of all privately held companies in the U.S. are
  owned or headed by women—10.4 million firms.

- Women's companies are more likely than others to stay
  in business, while companies owned by women of color
  are four times as likely as others to stay in business.

- Women's companies are creating jobs twice as fast
  as all other firms and pay more salaries than all of
  the Fortune 500 companies combined.

- Every day in the U.S., 420 new women-owned businesses are formed.

These numbers "defy logic," says Heffernan. Women
"receive only five percent of all venture capital. So not only
are women doing really well, but their businesses are thriving
when the playing field is tilted against them. That makes these
numbers all the more incredible."

Only 10 of the 500 CEOs at America's largest companies are women (hence their starting their own businesses!), but some companies are doing a lot better than the rest at promoting and retaining women at the top.

In March 2007, the National Association for Female Executives (NAFE) announced "The Top 10" and "The Best of the Rest" lists of top companies for female executives. IBM, Marriott International, General Mills, Colgate-Palmolive, Patagonia—for the whole list, go to nafe.com/pr_top30_07.php.

May I Suggest . . . Daydreaming with a Little Help from a Best-Of List

Feeling stifled in your current job? Feel you have talents that aren't being used? Check out *Fortune* magazine's list of the "100 Best Companies to Work For" (January 22, 2007 issue, money.cnn.com/magazines/fortune/bestcompanies/2007/index.html).

Times they are a changin', and so is the workplace. Making a living doesn't have to be a chained-to-a-cubicle grind, as the companies on *Fortune's* list confirm. The innovations some companies are making in the workplace will surprise you.

Browse and daydream, you'll soon remember that your work can and should be a place where you contribute and grow and, yes, even have fun. Who knows, the list may even inspire you to initiate changes in yourself and the workplace you're already in. Imagine.

A Couple of Unlikely Ambassadors
Take Their Good Talk to the World

The day after the 2007 Academy Awards show hosted by Ellen Degeneres, Degeneres appeared on *The Oprah Winfrey Show*. What was so remarkable, even newsworthy, about these two women appearing on stage together was that millions of people tuned in, enjoyed the show, and didn't necessarily think of it as a significant event.

But both Degeneres and Winfrey had overcome enormous obstacles to get to that moment in time. Winfrey is a black woman raised in poverty by her grandmother, on a pig farm no less, and Degeneres was one of the first celebrities to come out as being gay in a society that revealed it wasn't quite ready for it. Yet today they're both on *Time* magazine's list of the "People Who Shape Our World" and are as popular—one could even say beloved—as mainstream TV personalities can be. Their success stories illustrate that anything's possible. They also symbolize how far we as a society have come in embracing diversity.

Their TV shows are upbeat and empowering and they influence millions of Americans each day. And with large international audiences, Degeneres and Winfrey are also, in effect, a couple of U.S. ambassadors to the world. *The Ellen Degeneres Show*, which first aired in fall 2003, is currently broadcast in eight countries; *The Oprah Winfrey Show*, the longest running talk show in American history, has been on the air since fall 1986 and is watched by people in 132 countries—that's over two-thirds of the world—including Afghanistan, Iraq, and Iran.

Aren't we fortunate, then, that these two fine women represent the best of the American character. They're smart and funny and creative, tolerant, compassionate, and generous. Who might they be empowering today?

peace

noun / inner contentment, serenity • harmony in personal relations • freedom from war or violence • public security and order • a pact or agreement to end hostilities between those who have been at war or in a state of enmity • a state or period of mutual concord between governments • a state of tranquility or quiet

ci–vil–i–ty

noun / politeness and courtesy in behavior and speech • training in the humanities • the state of being a good citizen • orderly behavior • civilized conduct

---

With the Iraq war as the centerpiece of our daily news since 2003, and our local, national, and international news media persistently focused on stories of crime, violence, and political antagonism, it's no wonder that many of us are left with the perception that the world has never been in greater turmoil.

When we step away from the daily headlines, however, there's a heap of good news that paints a very different picture—one of a world that's becoming more peaceful and civil. Hard to believe, I know, but here's just a sampling . . .

Is War on Its Way to Becoming History?

A major new study reports that political violence has sharply declined worldwide since the early 1990s. The 2005 *Human Security Report* is a comprehensive survey of trends in warfare, genocide, and human rights abuses. Funded by Canada, Norway, Sweden, Switzerland, and the UK, the survey is produced by the Human Security Centre at the University of British Columbia and is published by Oxford University Press. It concludes that after nearly five decades of relentless increase, the number of genocides and violent conflicts has dropped dramatically since the end of the Cold War. It also reveals that wars today are far less frequent and deadly than in the past.

Three other major academic centers that track world conflicts also report a decline in global warfare and other conflicts: the Center for International Development and Conflict Management at the University of Maryland in College Park; the Stockholm International Peace Research Institute; and the International Peace Research Institute in Oslo, Norway.

Here are a few of the *Human Security Report* key findings:

- The number of armed conflicts has declined by more than 40% since 1992. The deadliest conflicts (those with 1,000 or more battle deaths) dropped even more dramatically—by 80%.

- Wars have become dramatically less deadly over the past five decades. The average number of people reported killed per conflict per year in 1950 was 38,000; in 2002, it was 600—a decline of 98%.

- International terrorism is the only form of political violence that appears to be getting worse. Data *had* shown an overall decline in international terrorist incidents since the early 1980s, but there was a dramatic increase after the September 11, 2001 attacks. The annual death toll from international terrorist attacks is still, however, only a tiny fraction of the annual war death toll.

- Wars between countries are more rare than in previous eras and now constitute less than 5% of all armed conflicts.

Why this encouraging trend? According to the *Human Security Report*, three major political developments over the past 30 years have contributed to the overall decline of war: the end of colonialism, the end of the Cold War, and the increase of international efforts, led by the United Nations, to stop ongoing wars and prevent new ones from starting.

The UN has received a lot of press in the past few years for its failures; its overall purpose and success have been called into question. The *Human Security Report*, however, gives the UN primary credit for the decline in wars. While the UN didn't act alone—The World Bank, donor states, regional organizations, and thousands of non-governmental organizations worked closely with UN agencies—it is, the report says, the only international organization with a global security mandate, and it has been the leading player in peace efforts.

A recent study by the RAND Corporation backs this up. It found that two-thirds of the UN's peace-building missions succeeded and that the sharp increase in peacemaking efforts resulted in an increase in the number of conflicts that ended in negotiated settlements.

Interestingly, 2005 polls reported that a majority of Americans turned against the Iraq war after roughly 1,500 U.S. combat deaths, and that a similar point in the Vietnam war didn't come until roughly 28,000 deaths. Is the reaction a result of this war in particular, or is there something else going on?

In a March 2006 paper delivered at the International Studies Association meeting in San Diego, John Mueller, political science professor at Ohio State University, suggested that war may be going out of style.

"War has greatly diminished over the course of the 1990s and particularly so during the last few years," Mueller said at the ISA meeting, "a remarkable development that has attracted scarcely any notice." War is an idea, he says, "an institution, like dueling or slavery, that has been grafted onto human existence." It's in general decline, he suggests, because our attitude about war has changed, "roughly following the pattern by which the ancient and formidable institution of slavery became discredited and then obsolete."

Which makes some sense. When the colonists first brought slaves to this country, they might have seemed so foreign as to be inhuman. But as time passed and slave and owner interacted

To read the full *Human Security Report*, go to humansecurity report.info. If you have teenagers, think about sharing it with them. The report is highly readable and it will certainly give your kids a more optimistic picture of the world they're inheriting.

To read John Mueller's paper, "This Just In: War Has Almost Ceased To Exist," visit http://psweb.sbs.ohio-state.edu/faculty/jmueller/.

day to day, that foreignness would have worn off. Once we see another's humanity, it becomes harder and harder to tell ourselves it's OK to enslave them. Today, as the world becomes smaller, "foreigners" become less foreign and thus harder to hate, enslave, or kill.

Attitudes change. Including those of a nation. In 1789, the U.S. had a Department of War. By 1949, its function changed and it was renamed the Department of Defense. Might the next step be a Department of Peace?

King Takes His Place with Jefferson and Lincoln at the National Mall

"We now have an opportunity to break the trend of memorials to war and erect a monument which delivers a message of lifelong peace in our land," John Carter, project chairman and VP of the Martin Luther King Jr. Memorial Foundation, said, in March 1998 to the Senate subcommittee that oversees the memorials in Washington, D.C. The Senate approved and, in 2005, voted to provide $10 million toward the $100 million needed to build and maintain the memorial.

The project is the creation and dream of Alpha Phi Alpha. Founded in 1906, it was the first African American fraternity; King was once a member. In 1984, George Sealey and

We do have a U.S. *Institute* of Peace. It's not a cabinet-level department, but it was founded and funded by Congress. Civics recap: The USIP was established in 1986 and is governed by a board of directors, which is appointed by the U.S. president and confirmed by the Senate. It was designed to be an independent, nonpartisan organization whose function is to "provide a unique combination of nonpartisan research, innovative program development, and hands-on peace-building support."

The USIP was the organization responsible for the Iraq Study Group, the bipartisan group co-chaired by former Secretary of State James A. Baker III, a Republican, and former Indiana Representative Lee H. Hamilton, a Democrat, which issued the *Iraq Study Group Report*.

In the first two weeks after its release on December 6, 2006, the report was downloaded from the Institute's Web site (usip.org) 1.5 million times and another 422,000 times from the James A. Baker Institute site. In spite of the fact that the download was free, the printed version still landed on bestseller lists, with Vintage, the paperback division of Random House, reporting that in just the second week, they were already into the third printing, with 250,000 copies in print. Clearly, the American public *is* engaged in what's going on in its government.

four of his fraternity brothers presented their proposal at the fraternity's board of directors meeting. Twelve years later, in 1996, President Clinton signed congressional legislation proposing the establishment of a King memorial in the District of Columbia.

A host of celebrities, musicians, artists, athletes, and authors have brought attention to the project—Oprah, Kenny "Babyface" Edmonds, Maya Angelou, Morgan Freeman, Whoopi Goldberg, and Carlos Santana, among many others—and as of January 2007, the foundation had raised $72 million of its $100 million budget.

The memorial, which is scheduled to open in December 2008, will cover three acres. Visitors will pass through two stones, representing the mountain of despair, to reach a third, the stone of hope, echoing Dr. King's 1963 "I Have a Dream" speech. (To take a virtual tour, visit the official Web site, mlkmemorial.org.)

Out of over 900 entries, the Roma Design Group won the competition to design the memorial. In a PBS *News Hour* interview (January 15, 2007), Bonnie Fisher, a partner in the group, discussed the concept behind the design. She explained that if we were to draw a line from the Thomas Jefferson memorial to the Abraham Lincoln memorial, the line would go right through the King site. Positioning the three memorials in this way reflects the connection between three great leaders of our democracy.

Crime Rate Reality Check

In 2005, the U.S. Department of Justice released the National Crime Victimization Survey, which came to this conclusion: "The rate of every major violent and property crime measured in the NCVS—rape or sexual assault, robbery, aggravated assault, simple assault, burglary, theft, and motor vehicle theft—fell significantly between 1993 and 2005."

Here are some of the report's highlights:

- The overall violent crime rate is down 58%.

- Sexual assault rates are down 69%.

- Robbery rates are down 57%.

- Aggravated assaults are down 64%.

- Household burglaries are down 49%.

- Thefts are down 52%.

- Motor vehicle thefts are down 56%.

- Property crime rates are down in every region: 56% in the Northeast; 50% in the Midwest; 51% in the South; and 52% in the West.

I don't know about you, but I find these statistics wonderfully shocking, they so greatly contradict our general impression of crime in the U.S. If the progress we're making were to become general knowledge, and was discussed widely, we would not only feel a lot better about where we are as a nation, we'd also gain new insights about what's working and why. We would then be in a position to apply our new knowledge—and see those crime numbers decrease even more. *That's* the real power of positive news.

Focus-Worthy Resource

Debunking the Scare Tactics

Why is so much news slanted toward the negative? Sociologist Barry Glassner offers some insights in his can't-put-it-down bestselling book *The Culture of Fear: Why Americans Are Afraid of the Wrong Things* (Basic Books, 2000). Among other things, he suggests that some cultural fears begin as a "false crime crisis" used by journalists to talk about other matters or to promote a certain agenda.

Did you know there has never been a single recorded incidence of a child being killed or seriously injured by tainted Halloween candy from a stranger? How, then, did the myth get started? And why do we continue to hear about it every Halloween? Glassner cites an October 28, 1970 *New York Times* article titled "Those Treats May Be Tricks" as the launch of the Halloween candy myth. "Those Halloween goodies that children collect this weekend on their rounds of 'trick or treating' may bring them more horror than happiness," *Times* reporter Judy Klemesrud wrote. "Take for example that plump red apple that Junior gets from a kindly old woman down the block. It may have a razor blade hidden inside, the chocolate 'candy bar' may be a laxative, the bubble gum may be sprinkled with lye, the popcorn balls may be coated with camphor, the candy may turn out to be packets containing sleeping pills."

No wonder our parents were in a panic. Even Dear Abby got into the game, cautioning against the perils of trick or treating. Glassner points to a 1975 *Newsweek* article that actually claimed, "in recent years, several children have died and hundreds have narrowly escaped injury from razor blades, sewing needles and shards of glass purposefully put into their goodies by adults," even though no deaths or serious injuries had ever occurred. (A fact confirmed by sociologist Joel Best, who conducted a study of every reported incident. And, as folklorist Jan Harold Brunvand points out, the idea that a person could put a razor blade in a piece of candy or fruit without making it obvious doesn't even make much sense.)

The Halloween scare surfaced in the 1970s—during the Vietnam war, the women's movement, and riots on college campuses—an insecure time, particularly for parents. The tainted-candy story, explains Glassner, like many scares, served a bigger purpose. It provided "evidence that particular social trends were having ill effects on the populace." A psychiatrist quoted in that original *New York Times* article actually stated that Halloween candy crimes were a result of "the permissiveness in today's society" and that "the people who give harmful treats to children see criminals and students in campus riots getting away with things, so they think they can get away with it, too."

Glassner explores other scares of our era, such as workplace violence, airline safety, child abduction, and road rage. His examples and analyses are fascinating. They remind us to question not only the reality of the various scares that crop up in the media but also what the possible agendas behind them might be. Because the real shame of these kinds of agenda-stories is that they contribute to a culture of distrust, neighbor suspicious of neighbor.

Literature Changes, and Sometimes Even Saves, Lives

In 1991, after a tennis game, Robert Kane, district court judge in New Bedford, Massachusetts, discussed with his tennis partner and friend Robert Waxler how disturbed he was with what he called "turnstile justice," in which offenders are sent to jail, eventually get released and wind up, again, before his bench, headed back to jail.

The comment sparked an idea. Waxler, a professor of English at the University of Massachusetts, Dartmouth, had been exploring the relationship between literature and society. "Let's try an experiment," he challenged Judge Kane. "Take eight to 10 men coming before you over the next few weeks, and instead of sending them back behind bars, sentence them to a literature seminar at the University. I'll get the room on campus, choose the books, and facilitate the discussions." The judge and a probation officer would also participate in the discussion.

Judge Kane agreed to the challenge, which took some courage, considering how his fellow judges would view this "soft" treatment. Waxler asked him to choose tough guys with significant criminal histories. "If this experiment worked," Waxler explains, "I didn't want detractors claiming that we had stacked the deck by choosing offenders with minimal records."

That fall, on the UMass-Dartmouth campus, the model for "Changing Lives Through Literature" was born. Over a 12-week period, on a college campus, a professor, a judge, and a probation officer came together with criminal offenders to talk about good literature.

In the first seminar group were, as Waxler had requested, "tough guys," 18 to 44 years old, with levels of education ranging from eighth grade to community college. (No sex offenders or murderers were allowed.) "They quickly got involved," says

Waxler, "offering some amazing insights into the stories. After the first series of seminar sessions, we knew we had to continue with the project. It was clearly making a difference."

The formula gives students confidence and teaches them how to think critically and make better decisions. Amazingly, the program has received accolades from all sides, left and right and in between. Both *The Humanist* and the *National Catholic Reader* have been approving of the program. "The program has stirred no visible controversy, partly because of what politicians of both parties consider a track record of success," William Bole wrote in the *National Catholic Reader* ("Books Better Than Bars When It Comes to Reforming Law-breakers," 1996).

Several studies of the program reported the following:

- The recidivism rate of Changing Lives Through Literature program participants is only 18.75%, compared to a control group of nearly 50%.

- Crimes of all types among CLTL graduates is 68% lower than among the control group; the rate of felonies is over 80% lower.

A year after Robert Kane and Robert Waxler began the CLTL program, Jean Trounstine, who was working as a humanities professor at Middlesex Community College in

Massachusetts and teaching writing and literature classes at Framingham Women's Prison, heard about CLTL. Soon she and an administrator from her college were meeting with Judge Kane to talk about beginning a women's CLTL program.

From her experience with women in prison, Trounstine knew that inmates are starved for activities. But, she says, "for women on probation, struggling to keep off the streets, I was one more responsibility to contend with."

As her new CLTL group met, however, Trounstine soon saw that the students were eager to come to the class and that the discussions meant as much to them as the reading outside of class. The assigned reading, as rigorous as any college course, includes complex short stories and novels from authors such as Hemingway, Steinbeck, Willa Cather, Toni Morrison, and Dorothy Allison.

"During our class time," says Trounstine, "the judge and probation officers looked at the women as thinkers—not as lost souls or tramps or washed-up mothers. But it is precisely because there are probation officers, judges, professors, and offenders in the group—the team concept so integral to CLTL—that the program participants begin to grow. The women feel recognized in a community where they have often felt scorned."

In 1994, with the help of the Massachusetts Foundation for the Humanities, the Massachusetts legislature awarded the first public monies to develop CLTL programs throughout the state. CLTL not only expanded throughout Massachusetts but beyond as well, to Texas, Arizona, Florida, Virginia, Kansas, New York, Rhode Island, Connecticut, California, and even England. The program has also expanded into prisons themselves.

Today over 4,500 offenders have gone through the CLTL program. Robert Waxler says that while the quantitative results of the program are important, "the change in the qualitative value of a life" is where the real value lies. And he has countless anecdotes.

"I recall one man, call him Anthony," he says, "coming into the seminar room one night after we had read Heming-

For the full interview with Robert Waxler and Jean Trounstine, see the Fall 2006 issue of *Mass Humanities*. (You can access it at mfh.org/newsandevents/newsletter/MassHumanities/Fall2006/interview.html.)

For more anecdotes, via text, photos, and videos, go to the Changing Lives Through Literature Web site, cltl.umassd.edu. You'll also find all sorts of information and resources for starting a group: sample syllabi, lists of texts, and teaching strategies, as well as a discussion of common challenges you might expect to encounter.

way's *The Old Man and the Sea*. Anthony told us he had been walking down Union Street in New Bedford, anxious and depressed, wrestling with his addiction, not wanting to return to drugs. He came to the corner near his old neighborhood, ready to make the turn. But he stopped, thinking about Santiago, the old man, and the battle he fought in the throes of his pain and suffering. It was as if Anthony heard the voice of Santiago at that moment. 'I thought if Santiago could endure what he did,' Anthony said, 'then I could walk down Union Street one more day, rather than make that turn into the neighborhood.' "

The Humble Book Survives, and Thrives

Every civilized society recognizes the importance that books and reading play in the quality of its citizens' lives, individually and collectively. As a publisher and a person who experiences regularly the power of good books—from great literature to scholarly nonfiction and everything in between—I'm happy to report that there are all sorts of indicators that say we are *not* becoming an illiterate pack of drones. We're reading. And maybe most surprising is that rather than taking away from reading, the Internet seems to be fueling it.

As for book sales, contrary to what some news reports would have us believe, they have been rising. The Book Industry Study

According to Scotland's national newspaper *The Scotsman* (January 9, 2007), on any given weekend at the John Radcliffe Hospital in Oxford, 67 children on average are treated for accidental injuries. On the weekends a new Harry Potter book is released, the number goes down to 36.

Oh, the power of a good book.

(By the way, according to *Forbes,* Harry Potter creator J.K. Rowling is the world's first billionaire author—encouraging news for English majors everywhere.)

Interested in finding or starting a reading group? These sites will point you in the right direction: readinggroupguides.com, bookreporter.com, teenreads.com, and kidsreads.com.

Group (BISG), the industry's leading trade association for policy, standards, and research, reports that publishers' net revenues for 2005 were $34.59 billion, up almost six percent from 2004, in spite of stiff competition from other, newer forms of entertainment and from used books. (The 2006 report isn't in yet, but estimates are that sales have risen again.)

"Are books in danger?" asks a *Forbes.com* special report on books (Michael Maiello and Michael Noer, editors, December 1, 2006). With competition from an ever-growing array of media, the Internet in particular, it would seem like the humble book doesn't stand a chance. "But surprise," says the report, "the conventional wisdom is wrong. Our special report on books and the future of publishing is brim-full of reasons to be optimistic. People are reading more, not less. The Internet is fueling literacy. Giving books away online increases off-line readership. New forms of expression—wikis, networked books—are blossoming in a digital hothouse."

Organized reading is on the rise as well. Diana Loevy, author of *The Book Club Companion*, estimates that close to

Kids are making progress in reading. In 2004, the National Assessment of Educational Progress (NAEP) administered the latest long-term trend assessment to approximately 75,000 students at ages 9, 13, and 17 in public and nonpublic schools throughout the nation. The 17-year-olds' reading levels had remained the same since the last assessment in 1999, but the 13- and 9-year-olds' levels are rising. Nine-year-olds are doing the best—the average reading score was higher in 2004 than in any previous assessment year. Indicating that efforts to get kids reading, over the past five to 10 years, are paying off.

For the full report, just type "The Nation's Report Card" in your computer's search engine and you'll be on your way.

20 million Americans belong to book clubs, many to multiple groups. The biggest of them all, Oprah's Book Club, has encouraged an enormous general audience to get excited about both classics and new titles—about 60 books, virtually all of which have become instant bestsellers, creating current-bestseller status for long-dead authors such as Tolstoy, Faulkner, and Pearl S. Buck. An amazing feat by any standard.

The book lives. We're reading. That's good news.

A Major University Shares Its Wares and Creates a New World of Knowledge For All

Five years ago, MIT, one of the world's most prestigious universities, began putting the contents of all 1,800 of its courses online, free to the world. Everything from course materials and syllabi, video and audio lectures, notes, even homework assignments, it's all there for the world, for free, at ocw.mit.edu.

It's called OpenCourseWare and MIT began the project in 2002. Its aim: to share knowledge with people beyond the confines of college campuses. It's an act of "intellectual philanthropy" and provides a new model of disseminating knowledge.

Companion sites are helping to translate the materials into other languages. Since the site's launch, MIT reports that there have been 36 million visits to the content.

"We're getting traffic from virtually every country on earth," says Stephen Carson, external relations director of OCW. "From a very simple but profound idea, OCW has grown into a global movement." The site is used daily by thousands of people worldwide. MIT reports that 17 percent of visitors are educators, 32 percent are students, and 49 percent are "self learners."

Now other colleges and universities are joining the movement as well. Some 120 or more from around the world—in the U.S., China, Spain, Portugal, Japan, France, Vietnam, and elsewhere—are sharing their courses.

And if that isn't amazing enough, rather than discouraging students from enrolling as regular students, MIT reports that the free online content seems to be doing just the opposite.

Bridging the Political Divide—A New Group Reminds Us We've Done It Before

There's no getting around it, relations between the two parties in Washington, D.C. have gotten just plain nasty. So much so that four former U.S. Senate Majority Leaders, two Republicans and two Democrats, have come together and formed a new bipartisan group. Launched in March 2007, the Bipartisan Policy Center (BPC) is on a mission to encourage across-the-aisle civilized and productive dialogue. The point being, it's time to get down to business and find solutions to our most pressing national issues.

Senators Howard Baker, Tom Daschle, Bob Dole, and George Mitchell are, they say, "dedicated to reversing the decline in political discourse and demonstrating that bipartisan policy solutions can be developed to address critical national challenges." They remind us, too, that this current state of acrimonious affairs isn't representative of a long slow decline; rather, it's more of a representation of pockets in history when we've lost our way before coming to our senses and righting ourselves.

In a March 5, 2007 press release, the group had this to say:

Reminiscing about Gerald Ford, Washington veterans marveled at how much less acrimonious were relations between Republicans and Democrats during his presidency, despite the Vietnam War and Watergate.

In the last 12 to 15 years, partisan animosity has approached that of the 1790s. At that time, anti-French Federalists voted to jail anyone who spoke in favor of France. (In the original draft of the bill, the penalty would have been death.) Jeffersonian Republicans responded with a threat to take their states, Virginia and Kentucky at least, out of the Union.

Partisanship in our time even calls to mind the 1850s, when a pro-slavery member of the House went onto the floor of the Senate to beat unconscious a Senator with an opposing view. From Richmond south, even professedly moderate Democratic newspapers lauded the action and urged dealing similarly with other abolitionists in the Senate and House.

In our time, while partisans have not quite gone to such lengths, communication across party lines has often resembled that between Washington and Moscow during the worst of the Cold War.

Fortunately, our current senators haven't starting beating each other unconscious yet. That's good news. But even better news is that perhaps the emergence of the BPC will give everyone involved—those in office and those of us watching them—the sound thump on the head we need to get moving in the right direction.

Just One More Example of Why It's Important to Pay Attention in History Class

There are few places on Earth where there has never been war, where the environment is fully protected, and where scientific research has priority. But the

> whole of the Antarctic continent is like this. A land
> which the Antarctic Treaty parties call a natural re-
> serve, devoted to peace and science.
>
> The British Antarctic Survey

In the 20th century, advances in technology allowed access to Antarctica, a vast continent whose inhospitable environment had up until then kept exploration to a minimum. By the 1950s, scientists from 12 countries had set up research stations, and nine of the countries had asserted territorial claims.

It was the Cold War period, tensions were high, and the United States and Russia were ready to lay claim to the continent. But instead of starting a territorial war, the two countries, along with the other countries involved—Argentina, Australia, Belgium, Chile, France, Japan, New Zealand, Norway, South Africa, and the U.K.—came together in a model of international cooperation and on December 1, 1959 signed the Antarctic Treaty.

The treaty's objectives are simple yet unique in international relations. They are:

- To demilitarize Antarctica, to establish it as a zone free of nuclear tests and the disposal of radioactive waste, and to ensure that it is used for peaceful purposes only

- To promote international scientific cooperation in Antarctica

- To set aside disputes over territorial sovereignty

The treaty remains in force and today 44 countries—representing 80 percent of the world's population—have become parties to it. Over the years, five new agreements have been added and are collectively referred to as the "Antarctica Treaty System." (For an explanation of all the agreements, a full history of the treaty, a list of the current countries involved, and all sorts of interesting information, visit antarctica.ac.uk.)

The treaty could be applied elsewhere today, says Donald Rothwell, a professor of international law at Australian National University. To the Spratly Islands, for example, "a collection of small islands and reefs in the South China Sea, where, like Antarctica, there is no indigenous population, and where multiple nations have laid claim over potential natural resources." Those laying claim to the islands, Rothwell says, could "engage in scientific research, without the tension of sovereignty . . . there's some chance of possibly acquiring the type of diplomatic and legal resolution of the issues that have been achieved in Antarctica" ("International Agreements Hallmark of Antarctica," *News Hour*, February 23, 2007).

Good news worth knowing and applying.

The World Just Got a Whole Lot Smaller, and Maybe a Little More Fun, Too

In 2005, media giant Rupert Murdoch and his News Corporation paid $580 million for MySpace, the Internet networking site made hugely popular by 15-to-25-year-olds. In late 2006, Google paid $1.65 billion for YouTube, the video-sharing Web site phenomenon.

Mainstream media has covered these two sales from all sorts of angles—among other things, lamenting the problems that the sites pose for parents; debating whether it's just scary that Rupert Murdock owns another huge chunk of media; and theorizing as to whether or not Google made an enormous mistake, considering that YouTube videos are riddled with copyrighted materials (all those songs playing in the background, for instance). When owned by two young guys without buckets of money, no one was running to sue for infringement. But with rich Google at the helm, would copyright lawyers swarm Google headquarters?

So why might we think the birth and rise of sites like MySpace and YouTube is good, even possibly great news for society?

Well . . .

According to a BBC News report, in August 2005, YouTube had 2.8 million users a month. One year later, the audience had grown to 72 million people. Think about that for a minute. People from all over the world, the equivalent of almost a quarter of the U.S. population, all visiting and interacting on one Web site.

Sure, there's some junk on YouTube and similar sites. It's certainly a legitimate concern for parents. But every form of media produces a certain amount of negative and nonsense content—even books—yet we don't condemn them out of hand. Take a look at YouTube's "most viewed videos of all time" and you'll see that the majority of entries are actually fun, informative, and inspiring. All that creativity, all that connecting and telling our stories. And all that involvement, people interacting and participating in an immediate way not possible with any other media.

Take, for example, "geriatric1927," the pseudonym of Peter Oakley from Leicester, England, a pensioner born in 1927. His five-to-ten-minute "Telling It All" videos, which debuted in August 2006, became, oddly enough, one of YouTube's most viewed videos and received all sorts of media attention. By the end of 2006, geriatric1927 was third on the Most Subscribed list, with 30,000 subscribers. An old gent widower living alone in London, how's that for giving voice to the masses?

And have you seen the wonderful "Free Hugs" video by Juan Mann? After the video appeared on YouTube, Juan landed himself on *The Oprah Winfrey Show*. That was on October 30, 2006. By January 2007, the video had logged nearly nine million viewings and Juan had spawned a worldwide Free Hugs Day campaign.

The free hugs idea flourished on YouTube with over 800 "free hugs" related videos appearing by January 2007. And interestingly, quite a few of the people posting their videos said they'd done the same thing a year, or two, or three before and had just never posted it.

One such video was posted by Hugh Mann (another "Mann," some symbolism there?), who explained, "Having seen the 'Free Hugs' video, I knew there was only one thing to do: Dust off the 6 DVD tapes I had waiting patiently to be edited since 2003, and get a long awaited project finished. Thank you for the inspiration, your video was the final push to get this done. . . . If you are inspired to do anything similar, you'll be guaranteed to have one of the most memorable days of your life! Post it on the Internet and pump it outside!!"

Hugh Mann's video, "Free Flowers!!!–Flowers4Peacein London," like Juan Mann's "Free Hugs" video, involves us. On the streets of London, Hugh set out to "bring a bit of peace and love to the planet by giving away flowers and cards to all he met." The story unfolds. As Hugh holds out his offering to young and old, rich and poor, black and white and every color, Dolly Parton sings "Peace Train"—*Oh, I've been happy lately, thinking about the good things to come, and I believe it could be something good has begun*—and, well, if that doesn't get you verklempt, I don't know what will. Watching it, you can't help but ask yourself, how would *I* respond if a stranger in a velvet jacket or a jester's hat handed me a flower in the subway station or wanted to give me a free hug at the shopping mall—what does my reaction say about my attitudes and assumptions about the people I pass on the street? What's surprising and inspiring is how many people do take the hugs and flowers, with pleasure, even outright joy.

And so *Time* magazine awarded the 2006 Person of the Year to "You," which many people felt was a cop-out, but was, on second thought, maybe, an important point. Because suddenly the power of the individual to influence others has expanded. Any one of us can be responsible for a "meme"—an idea, behavior, style, or word usage that spreads from person to person within a culture. In fact, the YouTube community concept, a meme in itself, has emerged elsewhere as more and more Web sites are using the idea of the meme to focus on a particular topic or theme.

Take, for example, Global MindShift, whose motto is "To change the world, change your mind. To change the world, connect with others." The organization's mission is "to help bring about a new era of cooperation and creativity on the planet," and it uses memes as a means of exploring and disseminating information.

A meme, says Global MindShift, is "a unit of cultural information that can be transferred from one individual to another. Like genes for the body, memes help cultures evolve."

The Global MindShift home page (global-mindshift.org) offers a variety of them to choose from, some created by the group itself, others submitted by visitors to the site. They range from short written pieces, like Scott Russell Sanders' essay, "The Most Human Art: Ten Reasons Why We'll Always Need a Good Story," to video clips and cartoons. My personal favorite is "Date a Brain" (written by Jason Ables, Richard Rathbun, and Kern Beare), a cartoon in which we learn about leading research that shows we humans have not one brain but three, each the product of a specific stage of our evolution.

In "Date a Brain," a young female contestant asks questions of three potential dates, each possessing one of the three types of brains. Guy Number 1 loves his cerebellum or reptilian brain. Muscle-bound and small-headed, when he's not running away from something, he loves to fight. Or mate.

Guy Number 2 loves his limbic or mammalian brain. Long-haired and peace-sign wearing, his goal in life is to do whatever feels good.

Guy Number 3 loves his neocortex brain, that most modern part of the noggin that allows complex, abstract thought. Guy Number 3 is smart and conscious and knows how to integrate his cerebellum, limbic, and neocortex. "He's got the whole package working in concert."

Our lovely contestant tells us she's looking for a guy who "loves a good time but knows when to be serious, is in touch with his emotions, but not ruled by them, has a global perspective, and lives a life congruent with what he knows." The audience waits in anticipation as she makes her choice. Entertaining and educational, this meme inspires us to consider how we as individuals and as nations are responding to the world. Are we using all three parts of our brains or still relying solely on old, outdated parts of ourselves?

Internet communities, memes, it's all about sharing our stories, sharing information, connecting. We blinked and the world got a whole lot smaller. Isn't that, just maybe, good news?

mind

noun / the faculty of thinking, reasoning, and applying knowledge • focus of thought, attention • opinion or desire for a particular thing or outcome, intention • disposition, mood • the collective conscious and unconscious processes in a sentient organism that direct and influence physical and mental behavior

body

noun / the entire material structure and substance of an organism • a person • the main, central, or principal part • a group of individuals regarded as an entity, a force • something that embodies or gives concrete reality to a thing

---

Traditional "health" news tends to focus on the latest disease or contaminated-food scare of the week. Add to this the proliferation of pharmaceutical ads and the picture is discouraging. Erectile dysfunction, acid reflux, insomnia, hair loss, pet allergies, dander allergies, more allergies . . . the message we receive, repeatedly and vividly, is that our bodies will fail us in specific (and often humiliating) ways. And when it does, our only recourse is the latest drug.

But that's not an accurate picture. After all, most of us today recognize the powerful connection between the mind and body—we know that what we think and believe affects us physically. So in this Mind and Body section, let's focus on the good news—positive trends and our changing perceptions about overall health, aging and beauty, physical activity, and the body's innate healing abilities.

We're Not Only Living Longer, We're Living Longer Better

Life expectancy in the U.S. has reached a record 77.9 years, and the gap between life expectancy for men and women is narrowing. For women, it's now 80 years; for men it's nearly 75.

Of course, living longer is really only good news if the long life we're living is a healthy one. We're in luck. A recent multi-university study led by Duke University Medical Center has concluded that older Americans enjoy good health for a longer period than previously realized, and that long spans of illness and disability are not necessarily part of normal aging. The study shows that a majority of people enjoy good or excellent health even past age 85. Later life is not necessarily defined by a steady decline in health, but rather by more healthy years followed by a short period of ill health immediately before death.

Funded by the National Institute on Aging, part of the National Institutes of Health, and published in the February 2006 issue of the *Journal of the American Geriatrics Society*, the study included nearly 3,500 men and women over 65. Between 80 and 90 percent of participants between the ages of 65 to 75 reported excellent or good health, so did approximately 60 percent of those over 85.

The study found that up to 50 percent of participants were free from any major disease; the rest were living with at least one physical ailment but continued to report at least fair health and had the ability to perform most of the activities of daily living. Occurrence of depression was also low—less than 10 percent. And nearly 90 percent of all the participants were healthy enough to live at home.

All of this contradicts the public's perception that the elderly experience a long slow decline in health, says Truls Ostbye, M.D., Ph.D., lead study author and professor in Duke's Department of Community and Family Medicine.

"We hear a lot about disease and disability among the elderly, but the quality of life in older individuals is actually, by most measures used, high, up to the oldest of age," Ostbye says. "Older people are healthy, and it is important for health providers to keep this optimistic perspective and share it with their elderly clients."

The Placebo Effect Confounds Researchers
and Points to the Healing Power of Belief

For years, the medical industry has been aware of the placebo effect. The debate may be ongoing as to comparisons between the effect of the placebo and the "real thing"—some studies say 35 percent of those receiving placebos experience effects, some studies say up to 75 percent—but the consensus is that the placebo effect is indeed real.

As Tamar Nordenberg explains in an *FDA Consumer* magazine article, "The Healing Power of Placebos" (January/February 2000), "Research has confirmed that a fake treatment, made from an inactive substance like sugar, distilled water, or saline solution, can have a 'placebo effect'—that is, the sham medication can sometimes improve a patient's condition simply because the person has the expectation that it will be helpful. For a given medical condition, it's not unusual for one-third of patients to feel better in response to treatment with placebo."

Which creates problems for pharmaceutical companies. "It's this powerful placebo effect," says Nordenberg, "coupled with the fact that many medical conditions involve a natural course of better and worse periods . . . that can make it difficult to know if a health upswing should be credited to a drug effect. One way to account for such variables in a drug study: give one group of patients placebo and another the experimental drug, and see if the drug group's health improvements sufficiently surpass those from placebo." The problem, Nordenberg explains, is that sometimes the tested drug fails to demonstrate superiority over dummy pills.

"The placebo effect has shown that beliefs are powerful, even those that are unfounded," writes Lynne McTaggart, in *The Intention Experiment* (Free Press, 2007):

> When a doctor gives a patient a placebo, or sugar pill, he or she is counting on the patient's belief that the drug will work. In effect, the placebo is a form of intention. It is well-documented that belief in a placebo will create the same physiological effect as that of an active agent—so much so that it causes the pharmaceutical industry enormous difficulty when designing drug trials. So many patients receive the same relief and even the same side effects with a placebo as with the drug itself that a placebo is not a true control. Our bodies do not distinguish between a chemical process and the *thought* of a chemical process.

Why is this good news? Because it confirms that the mind is a powerful thing, that what we believe affects what we experience, and that as a result, we have much more control over our well-being than we might have thought. With this knowledge, we're able to make more informed and conscious choices about how to maintain our health. It also gives us many more options should we find ourselves faced with an illness or disease.

West Meets East and Changes
the Face of Mainstream Medicine

While most of us have been busy with other things, a quiet medical revolution has been taking place. Over the past 10 to 15 years, alternative medicine has been slowly working its way into the mainstream medical industry. Mind-body medicine, often referred to as complementary and alternative medicine, or CAM, by medical practitioners, is now a normal part of most medical establishments, including government organizations.

The National Institutes of Health, the federal agency, for example, has a National Center for Complementary and Alternative Medicine, NCCAM, which introduces the topic this way:

> Mind-body medicine focuses on the interactions among the brain, mind, body, and behavior, and the powerful ways in which emotional, mental, social, spiritual, and behavioral factors can directly affect health. It regards as fundamental an approach that

respects and enhances each person's capacity for self-knowledge and self-care, and it emphasizes techniques that are grounded in this approach.

The most commonly used CAM treatments focus on intervention and promoting an overall level of good health and well-being. Some of the most often used are meditation, hypnosis, yoga, reiki, biofeedback, tai chi, cognitive-behavioral therapies, group support, and spirituality. Today, a cancer treatment that doesn't implement at least one of these alternative therapies is almost unheard of. Support groups and meditation are hardly considered alternative anymore, and hypnosis has proven to be, in many cases, an effective intervention for alleviating the pain from cancer and other chronic conditions.

Studies have shown that patients who go into surgery feeling relaxed and positive recover faster and require fewer, if any, painkillers, so many hospitals now offer patients relaxation treatments before surgeries. The Wentworth-Douglas Hospital in Dover, New Hampshire, has a Sail Through Surgery program that is typical of many hospitals today. It includes visualization, reiki, and music therapy.

Consumer demand has played a major role in the medical industry's transformation. A 2001 Center for Disease Control (CDC) survey found that nearly 70 percent of Americans have used at least one form of CAM therapy in their lifetime, often outside of the traditional hospital setting. The study also found

The following sites are just a few that offer interesting historical background and discussion of the various alternative medicines and their applications:

- The National Center for Complementary and Alternative Medicine: nccam.nih.gov/health/backgrounds/mindbody.htm

- Wentworth Douglas Hospital: wdhospital.com/services/patient-info/sail-through.php

- The University of Kentucky Colleges of Medicine and Health Sciences: mc.uky.edu/cam/trends_use.htm

- The Mayo Clinic: mayoclinic.com. Read "Complementary and alternative medicine: Evaluate claims of treatment success" at mayoclinic.com/health/alternative-medicine/SA00078. It offers a bit of healthy skepticism and guidance regarding some of the exaggerated claims made about certain alternative products and treatments.

that between 40 and 70 percent of CAM users still aren't discussing their use with their physicians, sometimes out of fear of disapproval. So, it's important to start communicating.

It's interesting, too, that the CDC survey revealed that CAM use has been greatest among women, people with higher education, and those who had already been hospitalized in the past year, a combination that suggests that intuition, knowledge, and experience are all part of the holistic health picture.

"Mind-body approaches have potential benefits and advantages," says the NCCAM. "In particular, the physical and emotional risks of using these interventions are minimal. Moreover, once tested and standardized, most mind-body interventions can be taught easily." They also can be very inexpensive, often free.

The mainstreaming of alternative medicine has several other positive side effects. It requires doctors to treat their patients in a holistic way, taking into consideration not just the symptom that brought the patient through the door, but the whole person—background, personality, beliefs, the big picture. And maybe most important, the medical world is more likely to discover effective treatments for various ailments and diseases when minds are open to *all* possible approaches. The emergence of a kind of "East-West medicine"—taking what works best from each tradition—gives us more choices and a greater potential to live full, healthy lives.

Have a Good Laugh, Meditate, You'll Live Forever

OK, not exactly, but study after study has shown that regular doses of laughter and meditation have measurable positive effects on the body.

For example, a study by cardiologists at the University of Maryland Medical Center in Baltimore found that people with heart disease were 40 percent less likely to laugh in a variety of situations compared to people of the same age without heart disease.

"People with heart disease responded less humorously to everyday life situations," says Michael Miller, M.D., director of the Center for Preventive Cardiology at the University of Maryland Medical Center and leader of the research team conducting the study. Those with heart disease generally laughed less, even in positive situations, and they displayed more anger and hostility.

Researchers aren't sure why laughing is good for the heart (though the rest of us have some pretty good ideas), but they do know, Miller says, "that mental stress is associated with impairment of the endothelium, the protective barrier lining our blood vessels. This can cause a series of inflammatory reactions that lead to fat and cholesterol build-up in the coronary arteries and ultimately to a heart attack."

Meanwhile, we may think of meditation as the antithesis of laughing, but the totally relaxed feeling we get after a long sincere laugh isn't all that different from the totally relaxed feeling that comes from meditation.

An 18-year study, published in the *American Journal of Cardiology* (May 2, 2005), concludes that a Transcendental meditation group (the practice includes muscle relaxation, behavioral techniques, breathing exercises, and quiet reflection) had a 23 percent reduction in death from all causes, a 30 percent reduction in death from cardiovascular diseases, and a 49 percent reduction in the rate of death from cancer.

The best news of all—both laughing and meditating are free, easy, and enjoyable while you're doing them, and their effects are lasting.

P.S. Study after study has shown that sex—yes, another free and enjoyable activity—is also good for our health. It reduces stress and can protect us against depression, colds, heart disease, and even cancer. "It does not take a degree in medicine to work out that sex is good for you," writes Lucy Atkins of *The Age,* "Anything that is free, feels fabulous and leaves you glowing is plainly a good idea." Enough said. Carry on.

Twice a week for best results, according to the experts.

Reality Struts Her Stuff Down the Runway

The scary-skinny models of the 2005 Madrid Fashion Week led to protests from doctors and women's rights groups. When the event rolled around again in September of 2006, the Spanish Association of Fashion Designers, in response to local government pressure, banned models who didn't meet their minimum standard body mass index, a measure calculated by dividing a person's weight by his or her height. They even offered medical treatment to excessively thin models. (Now *there's* a visual—medics lined up along the catwalk, ready to spring to action.) A couple of months later, Milan, the Italian fashion capital, also formally barred ultra-skinny models. They banned underage models as well.

Public response to the bans has been positive. Industry response, not surprisingly, has varied. *BBC News* reported that "some sections of the fashion world expressed outrage, citing discrimination against the models" ("Madrid Bans Waifs from Catwalks," September 13, 2006). The *Sydney Morning Herald* reported that Australians had a more positive response, with top modeling agencies coming out in support of the ban. Australians, one agency director said, "have a healthier attitude towards body image in that the lifestyle it encourages is outdoor activity and a lot more positive attitude" ("Body of Opinion Backs Model Clampdown," September 15, 2006).

Response from the U.S. fashion industry has been mixed, and the Council of Fashion Designers of America was not speedy in taking action. But with the pressure on, the CFDA issued some specific recommendations in January 2007, including that models identified as having an eating disorder should be required to seek professional help; that models under the age of 16 shouldn't be allowed to do runway shows; and that healthy meals, snacks, and water should be supplied backstage and at shoots.

Many have complained that the recommendations don't go far enough, aren't enforceable, and don't effectively address the body-mass-index issue. But the good news in all this is that the discussion is now well underway and on an international level to boot. Just in time. As one modeling agency executive points out, "In 1986, the standard size was 4 to 6. Then it was a solid 4 . . . Then zero." Clearly if something isn't done soon, only invisible will be beautiful.

It's hard to say what triggered this shift in perspective, but here in the U.S., the issue seems to have hit our radar around 2002, when Jamie Lee Curtis, at the age of 43, bravely posed in a national magazine in her underwear. She was protesting the fraud of photo retouching and the unrealistic images of beauty they perpetuate, particularly for young girls. (Those of us over 40 remember that while in her 20s, Curtis and her knock-out body starred in "Perfect." So at 40-something, she was the perfect person to reveal herself, and hence a little reality, in this public way.)

Curtis approached the editors of *More*, a magazine geared to women over 40. "I said to them, 'Let's take a picture of me in my underwear. No lighting, nothing. Just me. No makeup. No styling. No hair. No clothing'" ("Extremely Perfect," CBS News, August 2003). The photo got a lot of attention, of course. Women everywhere were grateful for the honesty. Relieved, too—the cat was out of the bag.

Other popular culture signs—movies like *Real Women Have Curves* and *Calendar Girls*—were also popping up, so that by the time Dove launched its "Campaign for Real Beauty," in summer 2005, with women size 6 to 14 posing in their undies, we were ready and, apparently, eager for it. Flipping through a fashion magazine, with page after page of prepubescent-looking, airbrushed models bearing little resemblance to 95 percent of us, it was refreshing, to say the least, to turn the page and see real women.

"When I first saw one of these smiley, husky gals" on a billboard, Seth Stevenson of *Slate* magazine wrote that summer, "my brain hiccupped. Something seemed out of place. Here I was, staring at a 'big-boned' woman in her underwear, but this wasn't an Adam Sandler movie, and I wasn't supposed to laugh at her. It felt almost revolutionary."

Stevenson's conclusion, overall, was that he liked what he saw. As to whether the ad campaign could be a success, he had little hope. "Because in the end," he said, "you simply can't sell a beauty product without somehow playing on women's insecurities. If women thought they looked perfect—just the way they are—why would they buy anything?" ("When Tush Comes to Dove," August 1, 2005).

Which isn't exactly a vote for the intelligence of women, but let's face it, we women (and men, too, admit it) spend a lot of money on beauty products we know aren't really going to change us. Good news for Dove, in that if we're choosing one nice body wash over another, knowing none of them can actually transform us, why not choose their product?

The debate over the photos has been active and ongoing, with the majority of responses being highly positive. In early 2007, Dove added more fuel to the discussion when it launched its "Pro-Age Campaign" using real women from 20 to 60, unretouched, with (gasp) wrinkles and *everything*. On NPR's *Day to Day*, Karen Grigsby Bates reported that Dove could already see that the campaign was a success and the company was receiving "rapturous e-mails."

"I saw that in person at a local drugstore while I was doing research for this story," Bates says. "A woman grabbed a big tube of body wash and tossed it into her red plastic cart. 'Is that good stuff?' I asked. 'I don't know,' she admitted; 'I almost don't care. I just wanted to support them because of their ads. Have you seen them? They're using real, grown-up women—and they are gorgeous!' " (Dove's Pro- [not Anti-] Age Campaign," March 27, 2007).

Oh, I know, we could be cynical and say Dove is just trying another angle to sell beauty products. But isn't it also possible that the women and men at Dove would like to sell products *and* help create a more realistic image of what beautiful, healthy women of all ages look like? (We tend to only hear about companies that behave badly, but Unilever, Dove's parent company, has a reputation for social responsibility.)

The positive response to the model/weight debate and the Dove ads are signs that perhaps our Extreme Makeover phase is on the wane. Maybe we're tipping toward a more realistic and attainable image of health and beauty. The fact that some other major companies are also changing their ad campaigns suggests so. Nike ads have been featuring close-ups of non-model-sized behinds and thighs and Bravissimo bra company recently began advertising with real, bodacious women of all ages. Some fashion magazines are taking the leap, too. The May 2007 cover of *Glamour* shouts: "The New Sexy Body! Healthy, Strong, and <u>Real</u>—women from 99 lbs to 230 show why every size is beautiful."

Mark Twain once observed, "A new thing in costume appears—the flaring hoop-skirt, for example—and the passers-by are shocked, and the irreverent laugh. Six months later everybody is reconciled; the fashion has established itself; it is admired now, and no one laughs." Throughout history we've

A little reality goes a long way. If you haven't already seen Dove's "Evolution" ad, go to youtube.com and type "Dove Evolution" into the site's search engine. If you have daughters, watch it with them. Sons, too. The film provides a vivid opening to what could become some liberating, perception-changing conversations.

gone to extremes in fashion and in our definition of beauty. In the past 20 years, we've seen images of women get skinnier and skinnier, younger and younger, flawless in a way that isn't humanly possible, and we've tried to keep up, spending enormous amounts of time, money, and effort, even enduring pain, to attain and maintain a fiction. But with any extreme, eventually we just get tired—or go broke. Then somebody holds up a picture, reveals the absurdity, and we're ready to move on.

We find ourselves looking back on those hoop skirts, beehive hairdos, and skeletal models, asking ourselves, What were we *thinking*? It's always up to us, though. Our response is what tips the scale.

Our Kids Got Too Big for Their Britches, Now We're Helping Them Slim Down and Get Healthy

It's not good news that many of our kids haven't been getting enough physical activity and have been carrying too much weight around. What *is* good news is that everyone from parents to school boards to local, state, and federal government organizations are stepping up to turn the situation around.

Schools all over the country are teaching kids to make healthier choices. They're implementing new fitness programs, eliminating soda machines, and providing healthier lunches. Some private foundations are getting involved as well. In April

2007, for instance, the Robert Wood Johnson Foundation announced that it would dedicate $500 million toward efforts to help kids lead healthier lives.

"Individual choice and behavior are important," says Risa Lavizzo-Mourey, M.D., M.B.A., president and CEO of the foundation, "but the world we live in plays a big role, too. We have to make it easier for kids to eat well and move more. That means more parks and safe places for kids to play, more grocery stores that stock affordable fresh produce, and improved school policies on nutrition and physical education."

The foundation's goal is to expand school-based programs, help states and communities coordinate their efforts, advocate for change, and evaluate impact. It will also encourage food and beverage companies to offer healthier products and change their marketing practices. "With this new commitment," Lavizzo-Mourey says, "we hope to foster more of these changes that will make it easier for families to raise healthy kids."

We took our eye off the ball and let our kids down, but we're awake now and taking positive action. By doing so, we're also feeding the overall trend toward a healthier American lifestyle: better food and less of it, more physical activity integrated into our everyday lives, less stress, more time spent with family and friends.

Let's take a look at two creative, forward-thinking programs, one in California, the other in Maryland, that are helping kids experience the fun and benefits of eating well and being active . . .

A California Middle School Transforms an Acre of Unused Land into a World of Healthy Learning

In 1995, a conversation between renowned chef and author Alice Waters and Neil Smith, principal, at the time, of the King Middle School in Berkeley, blossomed into something that continues to grow and flourish today—the Edible Schoolyard.

The project got underway when a one-acre asphalt parking lot was transformed into a garden and an unused 1930s cafeteria was refurbished to house a kitchen classroom. Today the school's Seed to Table program is integrated into the middle school's daily life.

When students start the program, the majority, like many in the general population, have little idea where the food they eat comes from, what's in it, or how it was grown. Following three principles—participation, ecology, and aesthetic—students plant, tend, harvest, cook, and serve the produce they grow. In garden classes, students get dirt under fingernails amending soil, turning compost, and harvesting the flowers, fruits, and vegetables. They learn, hands on, the principles of ecology, the origins of food, and respect for living systems. Then, in the kitchen classroom, they prepare, serve, and eat seasonal dishes they've created from their harvest. At meal's end, leftover scraps are returned to the garden where the cycle begins again.

The program teaches other skills as well. "Getting knee deep in the compost pile is not a first choice activity for any individual student," says Edible Schoolyard garden manager, Kelsey Siegel, "but jumping in together to turn the pile makes it fun and reinforces the importance of group work."

Siegel explains another benefit of the garden setting. "One of my continuing observations," he says, "is that the garden provides a place that helps level the educational playing field. It helps to subvert some of the disparities that occur within the classroom or even on the playground. In the garden, students have equal opportunity to take on the challenging jobs, to be loud and learn at the same time, to be active and energetic, or to be quiet and pensive. Through this kind of playful exploration in a group, students learn about the earth, each other, and problem solving."

During school, students are encouraged to eat the fresh produce grown in the garden rather than the usual sweet and fatty snacks. They're also encouraged to taste foods they wouldn't otherwise be exposed to. The health benefits, attitudes, and knowledge students gain reaches far beyond their at-school experience. You might say the Edible Schoolyard is growing up a fresher, healthier crop of kids.

The Edible Schoolyard is fully funded by the Chez Panisse Foundation. In 1996, Alice Waters, pioneering cook, restaurateur, and food activist, created the foundation in commemoration of the 25th anniversary of her restaurant, Chez Panisse, in Berkeley, California. Visit chezpanissefoundation.org for information, resources, and links.

A Baltimore School Lets Kids Prove to Themselves That Getting Fit Is Just Plain Fun

Eat your peas, they're good for you. Turn off the video game and take a walk, it's good for you. The "it's good for you" plea hardly works with adults—go to the gym, it's good for you—it's kind of silly of us to expect it to work with kids.

So how *do* we motivate them? One clever group in Baltimore has found an answer: Think like a kid and come up with an irresistible game.

In March 2007, third, fourth, and fifth graders in the Baltimore City elementary schools, nearly 500 kids in all, received backpacks filled with pedometers, log books, and bottled water. The game: record in your log book each day how many steps you've registered on your pedometers; the next day, try to beat your score.

At the end of each month, log books are checked and those kids who've been keeping up with the program receive an incentive prize. 50-inch TVs. Kidding. Get Fit Maryland wristbands or socks. At the end of the three months, students who finish the program will receive a jump rope and a certificate of completion, and the school that has the highest percentage of students participating wins the grand prize—a trip to an Orioles game.

Get Fit Kids is the latest version of Get Fit Maryland, an award-winning wellness program. It's a joint effort by the University of Maryland Medical Center, the University of Maryland School of Medicine, and the Merritt Athletic Clubs.

The focus of the program is not so much on losing weight as increasing activity, says program director Anne Williams, a nurse at the University of Maryland Medical Center. The program gets kids to challenge themselves and, by doing so, they also compete as a team member for their school against other schools, which gets everyone involved.

This book goes off to press as the kids are still breaking in their pedometers. To learn how the program went—and who won those Orioles tickets—visit the University of Maryland Medical Center's site, umm.edu.

youth

noun / the time of life when one is young • the early period of existence, growth, or development • a young person between adolescence and maturity • the quality or state of being youthful, associated with vigor or freshness • youthfulness

hope

noun / desire accompanied by expectation of • belief in fulfillment • one that is a source of or reason for hope
intransitive verb / to wish for something with expectation of its fulfillment • cherish a desire with anticipation • to expect with confidence • to desire with expectation of obtainment

---

"Kids today" . . . Since the first junior became a teenager, his elders have been shaking their heads and saying, "Kids, they aren't what they used to be." And yet, each generation of kids grows up and, surprise, the majority (that would be you and me) go on to contribute to an increasingly civil world.

Actually, the good news stories I've found indicate that "kids today" are getting it more right than we elders did at their age, which is doubly impressive when we consider that they're navigating through a world with more options and influences than the one we encountered. Our youth are our future, and as the following good news stories indicate, our future looks bright.

More U.S. Teens Are Saying Nope to Dope

The 2006 Monitoring the Future (MTF) survey of eighth, tenth, and twelfth graders indicates an across-the-board decline in drug use among U.S. teens.

- Illicit drug use among U.S. teens has declined 23.3% in the last five years, with reductions in nearly every drug, including alcohol and cigarettes.

- Marijuana, by far the most widely used of the various illicit substances, showed the fifth consecutive year of decrease among tenth and twelfth graders.

- Since the mid-90s, daily smoking among teens has dropped nearly 50%. In fact, many fewer of today's students have ever tried smoking than was true a decade ago.

- Eighth graders, the youngest students surveyed, have shown the largest proportional drop in their use of nearly all illicit drugs.

Since 1975, the MTF survey has measured drug, alcohol, and cigarette use and related attitudes among adolescent students nationwide. Designed and conducted by the University of Michigan and sponsored by the U.S. government's National Institute on Drug Abuse, it's the largest study of its kind, with 48,460 eighth-, tenth-, and twelfth-grade students from 410 public and private schools participating. In this 2006 study, students reported their drug use behaviors across three time periods: lifetime, past-year, and past-month. (For the official study results, including interesting graphs and charts to share with your own teens, go to monitoringthefuture.org.)

"There has been a substance abuse sea change among American teens," says John P. Walters, director of the Office of National Drug Control Policy. "They are getting the message that dangerous drugs damage their lives and limit their futures. We know that if people don't start using drugs during their teen years, they are very unlikely to go on to develop drug problems later in life. That's why this sharp decline in teen drug use is such important news: It means that there will be less addiction, less suffering, less crime, lower health costs, and higher achievement for this upcoming generation of Americans."

High School Students Are Making Brighter Choices for a Brighter Future

Since 1991, the prevalence of many health-risk behaviors among high school students nationwide has decreased, according to a comprehensive 2006 study. Black students are doing particularly well. They are less likely than white and Hispanic students to use tobacco, alcohol, cocaine, and other drugs; less likely to drink and drive; and more likely to use a condom if sexually active.

Fourteen thousand high school students participated in *The National Youth Risk Behavior Survey*, the results of which were released by the Centers for Disease Control and Prevention in June 2006 (go to cdc.gov/mmwr/pdf/ss/ss5505.pdf for the full report).

Renee R. Jenkins, M.D., professor and chair of the Department of Pediatrics and Child Health at Howard University College of Medicine, attributes these promising results to national, state, and local programs that educate kids about the dangers of risky behaviors. "These programs help kids develop social competency skills," she says. "Helping young kids contemplate better futures [helps them] make better choices" (*Black Enterprise*, March 2007).

And if that isn't good news enough, another report released by the Center for Disease Control in November 2006 gives us this:

- The teen birth rate in the U.S. has fallen to its lowest level ever recorded, 40.4 births per 1,000. The birth-rate for teenagers aged 15–19 has decreased 35% from its peak in 1991.

"The decline in teenage childbearing has been documented across all races and ethnic populations, but most impressive has been the decline in these rates for non-Hispanic black teenagers," says Brady Hamilton, a researcher at the CDC's National Center for Health Statistics and lead author of the report. The birth rate for black teens 15 to 17 years old has fallen 59 percent since 1991.

(I can't help but add this: There really was no "good old days when people waited until they got married to have sex." A major new study concludes that those numbers have remained virtually unchanged since the 1950s. "Trends in Premarital Sex in the United States, 1954–2003," was published in the January/February 2007 issue of *Public Health Reports*. "This is reality-check research," says study author Lawrence Finer, director of domestic research at the Guttmacher Institute. And it means we might need to adjust our thinking about today's generation of teens.)

One School Gets Big Results with Three New Rs:
Resources, Responsibility, and Real-World Experience

Cristo Rey schools—Catholic, though admission is open to students of all faiths—have an innovative yet simple approach to education and a very impressive success rate.

The program includes a combination of rigorous coursework, small class size, individualized support for all students, and a work-study program in which students are placed in entry-level jobs with local companies, including some of the nation's largest corporations—Best Buy, PricewaterhouseCoopers, Nike, Texas Instruments, and Blue Cross Blue Shield, to name a few.

Cristo Rey schools serve low-income youth in some of the country's most challenged areas. Ninety percent are Latino and African American, and the program deliberately chooses students who have not been able to "test in" to other Catholic schools in the district.

Students work one day for every four days in the classroom. The benefits are multi-fold. Employers pay the school 70 percent of each student-employee's school tuition (the remaining $2,650 is paid by parents, 60 percent of whom receive some aid). As a result, students experience the empowerment that comes with paying for a large portion of their education themselves. They also receive practical, real-world, white-collar job experience, develop work ethics, and learn the fundamentals of business behavior (how to dress and conduct themselves in a workplace, make eye-contact, all the basics).

In addition to gaining valuable job experience and marketable skills, students are exposed to a wide variety of career opportunities—a powerful thing for any student but especially for underprivileged kids. Students also develop a network of job contacts for the future. Doors and minds are opened. The result:

- The four-year dropout rate for Cristo Rey class of 2006 is an amazingly low 2.6%. (A 50% dropout rate isn't unusual in inner cities.)

- 99% of the graduating class of 2006 was admitted to a two- or four-year college; 95% enrolled.

The network currently operates schools in 12 cities across the country: Chicago; Cleveland; Denver; Kansas City, Missouri; Los Angeles; New York City; Portland, Oregon; Sac-

About 85% of the U.S. population now has at least a high school education, compared to about 51% in 1967, according to the U.S. Census Bureau.

ramento; Tucson; Waukegan, Illinois; and Cambridge and Lawrence, Massachusetts. In November 2006, the network received a $6 million investment from the Bill & Melinda Gates Foundation to expand to 23 schools, with seven scheduled to open in 2007 in Baltimore, Birmingham, Indianapolis, Minneapolis, Newark, Omaha, and Washington, D.C.

Cristo Rey's success begs the question: Could a version of this winning formula be implemented in our public schools, too?

Girls Take Top Prizes at the International Science and Engineering Fair, Again

What's all this we hear about American students, girls in particular, not being able to compete in science? At the 2006 Intel International Science and Engineering Fair, the Young Scientist Award, which goes to the top three students at the fair, went to three Americans, all young women.

What's even more encouraging is that all three winners in 2003 were girls as well. In fact, if we tally up the winners for 2003 through 2006, here's the breakdown: eight young women, four young men. Go, girls!

Held annually in May, the Intel ISEF is the world's largest pre-college science fair and brings together nearly 1,500 students from more than 40 nations. Students compete for tuition grants, internships, scientific field trips, and three $50,000 grand-prize scholarships.

And we're not talking about erupting-volcano models here. The work of the 2006 winners is impressive:

Hannah Louise Wolf, 16, Parkland High School, Allentown, Pennsylvania: *Sleuthing Epicenter Direction from Seismites, Cretaceous Wahweap Formation, Cockscomb Area, Grand Staircase-Escalante National Monument, Utah.*

Madhavi Pulakat Gavini, 16, Mississippi School for Mathematics & Science, Columbus, Mississippi: *Engineering of a Novel Inhibitor of Biofilm-Encapsulated Pathogens.*

Meredith Ann MacGregor, 17, Fairview High School, Boulder, Colorado: *Cracking the Brazil Nut Effect.*

To find out who won this year's Intel International Science and Engineering Fair and how you or your kids might get involved, visit sciserv.org/isef.

May I Suggest . . .
Serving Up Some Good News at Dinnertime

When I was a kid, my family ate dinner together, which is a great way to keep connected. Sometimes, however, especially when my siblings and I were teenagers and prone to bouts of sullen silence, conversation could be thin. If this is the picture at your dinner table, why not regale your family with a few good news stories. (Go ahead, steal from this book.) When you're finished, ask everyone at the table what good news they heard or experienced over the course of their day. The first night or two you're bound to get blank stares, but if you ask the question for a week or so, you'll be rewarded.

By anticipating—either consciously or subconsciously—that you'll be asking for a good news story, your kids will have their eyes and ears on the alert for good news. And if they're looking for it, they'll find it—good news breeds more good news. Make it a habit and you're on your way to creating a family of optimists.

A Student and a City Remind Us That Kids Are Both Resourceful and Resources

After reading an article about e-waste, 13-year-old Westerly, Rhode Island, student, Alexander Lin, got to thinking. Recognizing that old computers and electronics can contain metals and chemicals that create havoc with the environment if thrown into landfills, he wanted to do something to help. So, he gathered 10 other students together, and they researched the issue and came up with a plan.

First, the students sent out a survey to the parents of kids in the town's schools asking if they had old, unused computers and other electronics. Many did, but the vast majority had no idea how to properly dispose of them. So Lin and his group met with waste management experts and recyclers and conducted Internet research to devise a solution. They then held an "E-Waste Drop-off Day," refurbished computers they collected, and distributed them to 250 households that didn't already have computers. In addition, his group donated and set up computer centers for students in Sri Lanka, Mexico, and Cameroon.

All of this is impressive enough, but Lin and volunteers didn't stop there. The group made an educational e-waste PowerPoint presentation and went to elementary schools with it. They took it to their local town council meeting, too.

"Then," Lin says, "we drafted an ordinance to ban the dumping of e-waste and require safe recycling—and our town passed it! Next we went to a hearing and got the state to pass a law to require proper e-waste reusing and recycling in Rhode Island" ("Screen Saver," *Sierra*, November/December 2006).

Was it the PowerPoint presentation that was so convincing? No. "I think people took us more seriously than adults because they never see kids at the legislature," Lin says.

Indeed.

Now, imagine Alexander Lin's efforts multiplied exponentially. Like 17-year-old Geneva Johnson of New York City. She founded a youth service organization that works with inner-city kids to build pride and self-esteem. And 17-year-old Evan Ali-cuben of Hilo, Hawaii. He spearheaded a project that placed personal emergency dialers in the homes of nearly 50 senior citizens in his community. And 16-year-old Karoline Evin McMullen of Chesterland, Ohio. She co-founded Save Our Stream, a project that partners with student and community groups and with local and regional governmental agencies to clean up polluted streams and restore the habitat of the last remaining brook trout populations in Ohio. These kids' efforts represent the many creative and courageous things kids are doing all over the country and around the world to benefit their communities.

A few communities, in return, have recognized the powerful resource in their midst and are incorporating their youth into their town and city activities and planning. In Hampton, Virginia, for instance, youth are participating directly in the city government.

Hampton, a predominantly blue-collar city of around 146,000, has a modest average income and a youth population of approximately 52 percent African American, 40 percent white, and the rest mixed race. In 1991 the town's civic and political leaders did something pretty radical: they got their youth directly involved in the local government, schools, and community.

The town leaders "began to shift fundamentally the way they viewed youth," writes sociologist Carmen Sirianni in "Youth Civic Engagement: Systems Change and Culture Change in

Hampton, Virginia" (April 2005). "From seeing young people as bundles of problems and deficits needing the latest professional intervention recipe, city leaders began to focus on them as resources and assets to be actively engaged in contributing to the life of the community. They committed the city to a vision of youth empowerment and, in the years since, have continued to broaden and deepen the city's strategy to build a 'youth civic engagement system' seeking deep 'culture change' in the way institutions value the civic contributions of young people. . . ."

Today, says Sirianni, "Hampton provides the most ambitious case to date to institutionalize youth civic engagement across the city . . ."

In other words, instead of leading its youth, Hampton leads *with* its youth. The Hampton "three pathways" model integrates "service, influence, and shared leadership" so that with any issue young people care about, there are countless ways to engage them that create real benefit to the community.

If the city faces, say, a challenge with bicycle-related injuries, the three pathways would translate to something like this:

- As a service-learning activity, young people spend a Saturday morning teaching bicycle safety to children at a bike rodeo.

- To influence change, they advise city planners on dangerous intersections or new bike route designs.

- To share leadership, youth planners research, write, and propose a new bicycle ordinance for the city.

The result is that the city's youth, far from being "bundles of problems and deficits," are an asset, an invested part of the community.

"It's pretty unheard of for young people to have their own component (written by them) of an official city plan, as well as their own budget of $40,000 to fund programs," says Cindy Carlson, Hampton Youth Coalition director. "And in terms of impact, their recommendations have led to better, more cost-effective city decisions. Plus they are definitely more engaged in the community; Hampton has a 39 percent higher voting rate among young adults than the rest of the country."

Like Alexander Lin and his many community-minded peers, the youth of Hampton, Virginia, are the future. Very good news.

Focus-Worthy Resource

Youth Connecting with Youth to Get Things Done

Young people have that powerful combination of unfettered imagination, passion for topics that interest them, and confidence; they haven't yet fallen for the "certain things can't be done" trap many adults find themselves in. Which is why, of course, kids often *do* get things done.

They also tend to be Internet savvy and like to connect, so several useful sites have sprung up to help them do so. One of the best is YouthNoise. Launched in June 2006, it's a nonprofit, nonsectarian, nonpartisan organization, geared to young people from 16 to 26. The site's mission is to provide a place for civic minded youth to network and take their activism offline—"find, explore and network a cause" is the YouthNoise tagline. (Logging onto either youthnoise.org or youthnoise.com will bring you to the same interactive site.)

"We invite a young person to come in with a passion, and translate that passion into something they want to do," explains Ginger Thomson, YouthNoise chief executive. And they do. A high school student in upstate New York, for instance, organized a school blood drive, which netted 1,000 pints, then posted information about the project on YouthNoise, inspiring 18 other students to organize blood drives in their own communities.

The site's content is 100 percent youth-generated and is organized around 15 channels covering everything from War, Peace, and Terrorism, to Religion, Economy, Tolerance, Life, Art, Literature, and Media, with the ability to expand to any social issue the community chooses.

If you build it they will come. As of April 2007, the site has over 120,000 registered users, representing all 50 states and more than 170 countries. With an average of over 250,000 unique page views a month, that's a lot of positive connecting.

College Students May Not Have a Lot of Cash to Spare, But They've Been Giving Their Time in Record Numbers

According to the most comprehensive federal study ever conducted of college student volunteering in the U.S., 3.3 million college students volunteered in 2005. That's an increase of 20 percent between 2002 and 2005, with tutoring and mentoring being the most common volunteer activities.

In fact, volunteering by college students is growing at twice the rate of overall volunteering. Strong momentum, says the report, toward a national goal of five million college student volunteers by 2010. (Read the full "College Students Helping America" report at nationalservice.gov.)

Spring in particular is a big time for volunteering. College students get a lot of bad press during spring break, but there's a large and growing number who skip the beaches-and-drinking cliché and volunteer instead. Even MTV, famous for its (decidedly disturbing to parents) beach party coverage, has joined the call. "Spring Break is approaching, so check out what you can do now to plan an Alternative Spring Break," says MTV.com. "Experience one of the most rewarding weeks of your life!"

"The volunteer enthusiasm expressed by today's college students could have long-lasting societal benefits," says Robert Grimm, Jr., director of research and policy development. "Just as the Greatest Generation was shaped by World War II and the Great Depression, the tragic events of the last few years coupled with growing university and K–12 support for volunteering and service-learning have translated into more college students mentoring, tutoring, and engaging in their community in ways that could produce a lifetime habit."

In 2006, the first-ever President's Higher Education Community Service Honor Roll recognized colleges that have provided the most outstanding service to their neighborhoods and to the Gulf Coast communities devastated by Hurricane Katrina. The

College students interested in learning about alternative spring break programs, visit Break Away at alternativebreaks.org. Founded in 1991 by two Vanderbilt University students, Michael Magevney and Laura Mann, Break Away is a nonprofit organization that provides a national network for alternative break programs.

award winners for Excellence in General Community Service: California State University, Monterey Bay; Elon University, Elon, North Carolina; and Indiana University-Purdue University, Indianapolis. (For the entire list of winners, go to learnandserve.gov/about/programs/higher_ed_honorroll.asp.)

More than 500 colleges submitted applications, reporting that 219,000 students provided 2.2 million hours of hurricane relief support—making their parents, and the country, very proud.

heal

transitive verb / make whole or sound • cause an undesirable condition to be overcome • mend • cure • correct or put right • patch up a breach or division • restore to original purity or integrity • return to health

sus–tain

transitive verb / strengthen or support physically or mentally • keep in existence • give relief • supply with necessities or nourishment • nourish • carry or withstand a weight or pressure • prolong or keep up • support the spirit or vitality of someone or something

---

So, we've reached a consensus; global warming is part of our reality. With *An Inconvenient Truth*, Al Gore brought into focus what has been hovering in our periphery for years: we've taken the planet—a living, vital thing that has nourished us—for granted. Now it's time to heal and sustain our good Earth.

Clearly no one group or nation can solve this issue alone. Perhaps that's the gift it gives us; it requires us to communicate and work together for a common goal. As for Americans specifically, we're known for our ambition and ingenuity, now's our chance to prove it.

Many of us already are. Honestly, there's so much good environmental news—such a massive mind shift is taking place—I hardly know where to start.

But I'll try. Here's just the tip of the iceberg . . .

Companies Compete for the Green

Sustainability was at the top of the agenda at the 2007 World Economic Forum held in Davos, Switzerland, where officials said that rather than just awareness of global climate change, the next few years promise to be a tipping point regarding society's willingness to act on this awareness.

This shift in focus makes the "Global 100" even more sought after and relevant than before. Launched in 2005, the Global 100 is a list of the most sustainable companies in the world, based on ratings by an independent firm, Innovest. Companies included on the list must receive a AAA rating on their environmental, social, and governance performance. The point being that only companies who tackle these three issues will be able to sustain themselves long term.

Socially Responsible Investing, or SRI, is investment that integrates personal values and societal concerns. In other words, it's investing in companies that adhere to principles that are important to you.

The traditional investment industry promotes the myth that SRI funds don't perform as well as traditional funds, but there's no conclusive data pointing this out, and lots of anecdotal evidence indicating that SRI funds are at least, if not more, profitable than traditional funds. As the country and the world become increasingly socially and environmentally conscious, SRI funds stand to become even more profitable.

Interested in learning more? Get started at socialfunds.com.

Nineteen U.S. companies made the 2007 list, including Eastman Kodak, Nike, the Walt Disney Company, and Google. (For the complete list, go to global100.org/2007.)

The intended audience for the list:

- Investors looking for self-enlightened companies that plan to be around for the long haul

- Consumers wondering which global brands to buy

- Employees who want to work for a global company they can be proud about

- Managers who want to benchmark their company's sustainability performance

- Governments looking to attract companies that will contribute to building their societies

- Citizen groups that want to know which companies they may be able to work with in meaningful ways

So, in the end, doing the right thing really does add to a company's bottom line.

Smaller (But Mighty) Companies Making a Big Difference

A surprising number of the biggest corporations are thinking green and changing their ways. They are important examples for others in their industry. We don't hear as much about the many smaller companies, however, who are innovating and creating exciting new green services and products. So, let's give a few their due:

- Voltaic Systems, in New York, makes backpacks and messenger bags fitted with solar panels that can charge electronics, including cell phones and PDAs.

- Burgerville, a chain of organic fast-food restaurants with 39 locations in Oregon and Southwest Washington, runs on wind power and uses cooking oil waste to create clean-burning biodiesel.

- Hayward Corp., in Monterey, California, supplies construction contractors with sustainably harvested lumber, energy-saving windows, bamboo flooring, and insulation made from recycled denim.

- Interface, in Atlanta, uses recycled materials and biodegradable corn-based plastics to manufacture, of all things, carpet.

- Extengine Transport Systems, in Fullerton, California, retrofits old construction equipment and diesel-powered garbage trucks with a system that cuts smog emissions by up to 90%.

- IdleAire, in Knoxville, Tennessee, wires truck-stop parking spaces with hookups for heat and air conditioning, Internet access, satellite TV and movies on demand, so long-haul drivers can shut off their engines, saving fuel and reducing emissions.

- Prometheus Energy, in Seattle, captures methane gas from landfill sites and converts it into liquefied natural gas to power buses and other vehicles.

- EnerTech Environmental, in Atlanta, converts treated sewage into a renewable fuel that can be used as a clean replacement for coal.

- Verdant Power, in New York, is developing submergible turbines that convert the power of natural tides and currents from New York's East River into household electricity.

- Excellent Packaging and Supply, of Richmond, California, distributes compostable and biodegradable utensils and food packaging, for your next picnic.

- Zoots, an 80-store dry-cleaning chain based in Newton, Massachusetts, uses only 100% bio-degradable fluids (instead of perchloroethylene, the industry standard).

- Frog's Leap, in Rutherford, California, produces around 60,000 cases of wine a year using organically grown grapes and a water-saving, dry-farming technique.

- NaturaLawn America, in Frederick, Maryland, uses natural fertilizers and weed inhibitors and an integrated pest management system that lets beneficial insects keep harmful ones under control.

- And when it's time to go, Memorial Ecosystems, in Westminster, South Carolina, who gave us the nation's first green cemetery, offers simple funeral services without using embalming fluids or other harmful chemicals, hardwood caskets, or conventional headstones.

Healthy Competition Creates Solutions

In an effort to find solutions to the issue of contaminated drinking water, a problem that affects millions of people worldwide, the Grainger Foundation, through the National Academy of Engineering (NAE), set a $1 million challenge.

Contaminated drinking water is a major cause of child mortality in Third World countries. Arsenic is often the culprit. Although arsenic compounds are a naturally occurring species, they only become a problem when they are water soluble, especially in groundwater used for drinking. When communities in wealthy nations, like the U.S., have high doses of arsenic in their water sources, they install expensive, centralized cleanup technologies. In poor countries, this isn't an option.

With that in mind, the 2007 Grainger Challenge Prize for Sustainability set specific criteria for the challenge: the filtration systems had to be affordable, reliable, easy to maintain, socially acceptable, and environmentally friendly.

From more than 70 entries, the first prize went to Abul Hussam, an associate professor in the department of chemistry and biochemistry at George Mason University, Fairfax, Virginia, who was born in Kushtia, Bangladesh. Hussam won the $1 million prize for his SONO filter, a household water system. (Read about the other winners and their solutions at nae.org.)

OneWorld South Asia reports that Hussam spent years testing hundreds of prototype filtration systems. His final innovation is a simple, maintenance-free system that uses sand, charcoal, bits of brick and a porous composite iron matrix. Each filter has about 5 kilograms of porous iron, which forms a chemical bond with arsenic. (For a good visual of how the SONO filter works, go to http://chemistry.gmu.edu/faculty/hussam/handouts/AS_filtration.pdf.)

About 200 of the SONO filtration systems are now being made each week in Kushtia, for about $40 each, Hussam says. More than 30,000 SONO units have been distributed so far.

Hussam's not done contributing to the solution. He says he plans to use 70 percent of his prize to distribute filters to needy communities; 25 percent will be used for more research; and five percent will be donated to George Mason University.

Golf Course Pond Provides Dinner and Wins an EPA Award

When the chefs of the Four Seasons Resort Hualalai on the Kailua-Kona coast of Hawaii's Big Island need fish or shrimp for a recipe, they only have to travel as far as the fifth hole on their Ke'olu Golf Course.

Lake Punawai is a three-million gallon, 2.5 acre, 10-foot deep "living machine." It's an example of phytoremediation, the treatment of environmental problems using plants. The lake was built to be clean, energy efficient, and visually pleasing, and to supply the resort's restaurant with fish. It's stocked with moi, mullet, milkfish, and Pacific White Shrimp. Oysters live in the pond, too, but for filtration purposes only, not dinner.

Four Seasons partnered with Natural Systems Inc. and Ocean Arks International to create Lake Punawai. It's lined with a foot of gravel and features two floating islands of plants that, with the help of a three-horsepower pump to circulate the water, remove pollution and excess nutrients from the water.

The lake also saves the resort a lot of energy and, therefore, money. "If we set up another area as a fish pond without this system," explains David Chai, the resort's director of natural resources, "it would cost close to $10,000 a month in power—this one runs about $400" ("Living Machine," *West Hawaii Today*, April 22, 2005).

At the 2005 Environmental Awards Ceremony, the EPA recognized Four Seasons Resort Hualalai for Lake Punawai, citing that the lake promotes an innovative idea, addresses environmental problems over the long term, and can be replicated in other places.

"When the EPA looked at this project," said Dean Higuchi, EPA press officer in Honolulu, "we saw a good example of how a business can interact with the environment and turn it into something positive for both their operations and natural resources."

One of the World's Largest Wetland Ecosystems Is on the Road to Recovery

In 2001, the United Nations Environment Programme (UNEP) alerted the international community to the destruction of the Iraqi Marshlands when it released satellite images of the area showing that 90 percent of the Marshlands had been lost. New satellite images released in December 2006 show that 50 percent of the marshlands are now re-flooded. An amazing comeback in just five years.

Extensive ecological damage to this area, with the accompanying displacement of much of the indigenous population, was identified as one of the country's major environmental and humanitarian disasters. Today, according to the UNEP, up to 300 Iraqis have been trained in marshland management techniques and policies, and up to 22,000 people living in the area now have access to safe drinking water.

The project, "Support for Environmental Management of the Iraqi Marshlands," is managed by the UNEP. "The key to the success of this project has been the solid cooperation with Ministries of Environment and Municipalities and Public Works, southern Governorates, local communities . . . and the dedication of many Iraqis," said Per Bakken, director of the UNEP International Environmental Technology Centre. A series of community-led environmental awareness campaigns were organized by local leaders and residents, and an Internet-based Marshland Information Network has been set up as well.

Now that the first phase of the project has proven so successful, phase two is underway. Its focus is on data collection, water analysis, and further technical training and awareness raising.

This marshland comeback is similar to many environmental recoveries we see around the world. Once we focus on an issue and take action, Mother Nature often, perhaps in appreciation, responds with amazing speed.

Oh, The Power of Poop

In 2005, British Columbia's capital city of Victoria was the only major city in Canada that did not have some type of formal sewage treatment. With 34 million gallons of raw sewage being dumped daily into the Strait of Juan de Fuca, concerned citizens and environmentalist had tried—with everything from lobbying to suing—to get public officials to take action, to no avail.

Enter Mr. Floatie, a six- (some reports say seven-) foot poop with a falsetto voice. (OK, it's not a real poop. Just a young activist named James Skwarok in a disturbingly convincing brown suit.)

Mr. Floatie made his first appearance at a Victoria-Hillsdale district candidates' meeting in British Columbia's May 2005 provincial election, before making other public appearances around the city.

Apparently, the power of a six-foot poop cannot be denied. The BC Ministry of the Environment ordered the city to cease its dumping by June 2007.

Meanwhile, baby poop has motivated one creative mother to take the situation in hand. Diapers are non-biodegradable, and some estimates say they can take up to 100 years to break down. The good news: Marlene Sandberg, a lawyer and mother in Sweden, has developed Nature Babycare diapers, made of chlorine-free wood pulp and corn-based film, all biodegradable. They're already available in Sweden, the Netherlands, Belgium, Australia, and England. And soon to be available in the U.S.

Not to be outdone, a duo in Wales has developed a new use for something they have plenty of. Yup, sheep poop. As explained on the Creative Paper Wales site (creativepaper wales.co.uk): "Sheep Poo Paper is the ultimate in environmental entrepreneurialism. It takes a waste product no one wants, transforms it into beautiful products, and even sells its washing water as fertilizer. Nothing is wasted, nothing is degraded, nothing is damaged." And not to worry, the poo is completely sterilized.

Founders Lawrence Toms and Lez Paylor "had been keen to develop an idea which would create a manufacturing company which would be uniquely Welsh and could produce a product that foreign imports could not compete with" ("Sheep Poo Paper Scoops Top Award," BBC News, September 7, 2006). Their efforts and creativity have paid off. In August 2006, they were awarded a £20,000 Millennium Award for social entrepreneurship.

From "Birthday Bleating" and "I Love Ewe" cards to Sheep Poo Airfresheners, Creative Papers Wales has something for every pooper, er, paper need.

Helping the World's Forests Tip the Right Way

An international team of experts from diverse disciplines and following independent lines of thinking has concluded that the outlook for the world's forests is promising. In a paper published in the *Proceedings of the National Academy of Sciences*, the team reports that the world could be approaching a turning point from deforestation.

The study, "Returning Forests Analyzed with the Forest Identity," shows that forests of Earth's two most populated nations no longer increase atmospheric carbon concentration: China's forests are expanding; India's have reached equilibrium. And although the Asian continent lost nearly two million acres between 1990 and 2000, it gained nearly 2.5 million acres between 2000 and 2005—an amazing increase for such a short period. In addition, over the past 15 years, forest stock has expanded in 22 of the world's 50 most forested nations. (For the full report, go to pnas.org/cgi/content/full/103/46/17574.)

"Earth suffered an epidemic of deforestation. Now humans may help spread an epidemic of forest restoration," says Jesse H. Ausubel, study co-author and environmental scientist. "This great reversal in land use could stop the styling of a Skinhead Earth and begin a great restoration of the landscape by 2050, expanding the global forest by 10 percent—about 300 million hectares [around 740 million acres], the area of India."

The forest gains, says the study, are due in large part to urban migration, increase in crop yields (better agricultural practices that require the use of less cleared land), and effective reforestation policies. Also helping are new tree plantations, which supply timber for products such as paper, rather than cutting old-growth forests. The study predicts that by 2025, the share of industrial wood production coming from forest plantations will increase from one third to half, and that by 2050, it will have increased to three-quarters.

In an effort to help tip forests the right way, 125 U.S. publishers, mostly small and medium sized, have signed the Treatise on Responsible Paper Use, pledging, among other measures, that by 2011, they'll use an annual average of 30-percent post-consumer recycled fiber for their book printing. The treatise is the work of the Green Press Initiative, a non-profit organization whose mission is "to work with publishers, industry stakeholders, and authors to create paper-use transformations that will conserve natural resources and preserve endangered forests." Representatives from 30 publishers, paper mills, and printers helped to develop the treatise (which you can read at greenpressinitative.org, along with the list of publishers who've signed it).

Random House, the world's largest trade publisher, stepped up in May 2006 and pledged that by 2010, at least 30 percent of the uncoated paper it uses to print the majority of its U.S. titles will be derived from recycled fibers.

To put the Random House initiative in perspective, the estimated environmental impact of this recycling commitment, at its full implementation in 2010, will equate to the preservation of more than 550,000 trees a year, reducing harvesting requirements by over 80,000 tons of timber annually. It's a big move and many in the industry expect that it will prompt other large publishers to step up as well.

> Moment Point Press, the very small (but mighty) publisher, not only signed the Green Press Initiative treaty, but since our founding in 1998, we've printed 80% of our books on 50% post-consumer recycled paper, including the book you're holding.

Giving a Green Gift on a Golden Anniversary

As it approached its 50th anniversary, Enterprise Rent-A-Car wanted to make a significant gift for the next 50 years, something that would have a meaningful connection to its business, its employees, and the communities it serves. With a nudge from The National Arbor Day Foundation (NADF), the company announced in 2006 that it would give NADF

$50 million over the next 50 years to plant 50 million trees.

Each year, NADF will identify a number of tree planting projects throughout the U.S. and work with similar agencies in Europe and Canada. Enterprise will then fund the planting of a million trees in the areas determined to need them most. The hardworking men and women at the U.S. Forest Service will do the actual planting.

One million trees planted this year, when they reach maturity, will absorb 15,000 tons of CO_2 and produce 10,000 tons of oxygen per year—enough to meet the needs of 45,000 people, according to The National Arbor Day Foundation.

"To put this gift in perspective, 50 million trees is the equivalent of planting a new Central Park about every 10 days, all year, for the next 50 years," said Andy Taylor, Enterprise Chairman and CEO. "We know this commitment is not a total solution, but it's a solid step in the right direction."

The World Cup Scores One for the Environment

According to the United Nations Environment Programme (UNEP), the 2006 30-day soccer tournament held in Germany will go down in history as the first "climate neutral" World Cup (see unep.org).

"The German Local Organizing Committee has put down a clear and unequivocal environmental foundation from which future host countries can now build," the head of the UNEP said at the launch of a final report on the achievements of the "Green Goal," an initiative undertaken by the German organizers of the Féderation Internationale de Football Association (FIFA) 2006 World Cup.

Stadium waste was reduced by 17 percent, in part due to campaigns like "Put It in a Roll," aimed at minimizing the use of paper plates and cardboard containers, and the "Cup o the Cup," a returnable cup for beer and soda. Initiatives, by the way, that could be easily implemented at any stadium.

Water consumption was lowered by 20 percent due in part to the use of water-saving toilets and rainwater harvesting systems. Organizers set themselves a target that 50 percent of journeys to and from stadiums would be by public transportation; they beat their target by over seven percent.

"Unlike the Olympics, the environment has been something of an outsider at World Cups, but this has now changed and to my mind there is no going back," said Achim Steiner, UN under-secretary general and UNEP executive director. "Organizers of future FIFA World Cup events will now have to consider playing the environment up front as one of the leading strikers in their planning and policy strategies. Otherwise they risk 'own' goals and off-sides from domestic and international public opinion."

Proving once again that competition is a great environmental motivator.

Eco-tourism Turns the Page

"Note to consumers: if you're looking for *the* definitive book on 'green' travel, you won't find it," says a *Publishers Weekly* cover story ("Going with the Green," January 29, 2007). "Publishers are no longer promoting anything approximating 'The Definitive Book on Green Travel.' Instead, they've responded to consumer needs: releasing guide-book series that incorporate green- and eco-travel sections, creating resources around principles of sustainability, and using production methods in keeping with those principles." Even the most mainstream travel guides are incorporating green travel into their travel books, and the sections are expanding.

As for travel itself, according to the Travel Industry Association of America, 83 percent of U.S. travelers are willing to spend more for travel services and products provided by environmentally responsible companies.

There are nearly 100 eco-travel groups with their own specific sets of standards when it comes to defining eco-tourism. But, no need to be confused, the International Ecotourism Society (ecotourism.org) defines ecotourism simply enough: "Responsible travel to natural areas that conserves the environment and improves the well-being of local people."

Whether you choose to explore the natural wonders of the U.S. or venture farther afield, here's an example of how an eco-vacation can benefit the people of a region as well as animals and their habitat.

There are approximately 700 surviving mountain gorillas in the wilds of Rwanda, Uganda, and the Democratic Republic of Congo. Although nearly poached into extinction, a new census shows the mountain gorilla population grew by 17 percent between 1989 and 2003 (2003 being the last year for which there is data). According to the chief park warden of Rwanda's Parc National Des Volcans, there hasn't been a difference in the number of births. What has changed is the dedicated anti-poaching and conservation efforts, which include close monitoring and working with locals to protect the habitat.

It seems counterintuitive, but what may be helping the mountain gorilla population is the tourist industry.

In Rwanda, foreign visitors pay $375 for the experience of visiting the gorillas in their natural habitat, though with strict rules, including keeping at a certain distance. Each day a maximum of eight people are allowed to visit one of seven groups of gorillas and stay for just one hour. The gorillas have become accustomed to receiving visitors.

With hundreds of tourists visiting every month and more wanting to come, it adds to the Rwandan government's incen-

U.S. ski resorts are taking action. At least 57 resorts in 16 states are now buying clean energy—including hydroelectric, wind, solar, geothermal, and bio-mass. They're also pushing global warming legislation in Washington.

In September 2006, the National Ski Areas Association (NSAA) launched a Green Power Program, which includes an "Environmental Code of the Slopes" and "Keep Winter Cool" program. Visit nsaa.org to find out which slopes are doing their part and pick up some tips on how to make your next ski-trip more eco-friendly.

When spring arrives and it's time to get out the clubs, golfers can support courses that are protecting the environment, conserving water, and proving wildlife habitat. Just go to golfandenvironment.org, click on Take Action and then Support Your Golf Course. Along with the helpful tips, the site will also help you find an Audubon-Certified, environmentally friendly course near you.

tive to protect this precious natural resource. "Gorillas are our national pride," said guide Francis Bayingana. "There has to be promotion of conservation."

So, planning a vacation? In addition to the great new guidebooks out there, also check out environmentally friendlyhotels.com. It will help you find hotels, bed and breakfasts, inns, and resorts worldwide that are committed to the environment. You'll be surprised by the operations that are already green.

Don't forget to get the kids involved in the planning. They'll learn a lot and, who knows, you may have a little Eco-travel Agent in the making.

Focus-Worthy Resources

Green Tips at Our Fingertips

Paper or Plastic? Halogen or Incandescent? Is it me or does it all get a bit confusing? We all want to do what's best for the environment, but sometimes knowing *what's* best is a mystery. In my good news search, I've discovered some excellent resources to help us be good green citizens. Because, really, with a little guidance, it's easy being green.

If you're a book and print lover, you'll appreciate having the following two magazines around the house. Both present environment-related news stories, national and international, mixed with tidbits of practical information—a nice balance of the good and bad of it. They're both bi-monthly (so not too overwhelming if you're a very busy bee), visually appealing, printed on recycled paper, and, hint, like *Ode* mentioned earlier, they're good magazines to leave lying around for your teenagers.

Sierra **magazine**—"Explore, Enjoy, and Protect the Planet": Includes an "Innovators" section highlighting "imaginative and sometimes quirky geniuses who roll up their sleeves and use technology to solve some of our most pressing environmental issues"; and a "Sustainability Is Stylish" section with practical tips for our everyday lives. *Sierra* keeps us abreast of what's happening in Washington, too. It's $15.00 for a year's subscription, or make a donation and it's part of your membership. sierraclub.com/sierra or call 415-977-5500.

Plenty **magazine**—"It's Easy Being Green": In addition to its big, pretty magazine layout, *Plenty* has a meaty (rather impressive, actually) Web site, with podcasts, TV, blogs— you can go to town if you're so inclined. $12.00 per year, plentymag.com or call 800-316-9006.

For green tips conveniently delivered daily to your email-box, don't miss:

IdealBite.com—"A Sassier Shade of Green": Co-founders Heather Stephenson and Jennifer Boulden understand human nature: "People simply don't want to be told what's wrong, without being told how they can realistically help." So they gathered a team of experts in fields as varied as interior design, food and drink, household goods, even pets, to provide "Daily

Bites," environmental tips that apply to every aspect of our lives. From beauty products to burial tips, they cover it all, with useful information that's not only practical but raises our consciousness about the autopilot things we do everyday.

What really sets this site apart is the encouraging tone and way the information is presented. The *Ideal Bite* crew has a sense of humor and they make us feel that we can, indeed, make small changes that will add up. No guilt, no shame, just practical tips we can apply. "Small changes, done by many, create big results" is their motto.

Give *Ideal Bite* your email address (takes all of five seconds) and each day you'll receive an email with a pithy bite. Like this one, for example:

Question: Paper or plastic?

The Bite

Answer: Neither. Shopping bags create an insane amount of waste for something that's often in our lives for fewer than five minutes (store to car, car to house). Next time you grocery shop, BYOB (bring your own bag).

The Benefits

- Save oil and/or trees. In the U.S., about 12 million barrels of oil and 14 million trees go to producing plastic and paper bags each year.

- Reusing makes cents. Stores like Albertsons and Wild Oats offer a five-penny discount if you bring your own.

- Be a role model. Other shoppers'll watch and learn.

- Make sure plastic bags don't harm sea creatures. They're one of the 12 most commonly found items in coastal cleanups. If you can't get around using plastic bags, tie them into knots before you toss them in the recycle bin. That way they won't balloon up into the air and end up as litter.

- If 10,000 Biters use canvas totes instead of plastic grocery bags, we'll keep about nine million bags from ending up in landfills every year.

10 More Miles Could Get Us Out of the Persian Gulf

Though we must think BIG when it comes to ridding ourselves of oil dependency, it's surprising how little would make a big difference. In an article covering the Los Angeles Auto Show, Jason Mark of the Union of Concerned Scientists tells the *Christian Science Monitor* that if cars throughout the U.S. could get an average of just 10 miles more per gallon than they are currently, the savings would be 2.3 million barrels of oil a day, the equivalent of our current Persian Gulf imports.

The auto show featured 21 alternative-fuel vehicles. Said *Automobile* magazine editor in chief, Gavin Conway, "the overriding concern this year is the environment" ("On the Road to Clean Fuels," *Christian Science Monitor*, December 1, 2006).

According to the 2007 Fuel Economy Guide (at fueleconomy.gov), hybrid cars dominate the list of the most fuel-efficient vehicles. The guide awards first and second place to Toyota's Prius, logging 60 city/51 highway miles per gallon, and Honda's Civic Hybrid, logging 49/51. Both are gas/electric hybrids. They run on regular gas and, though their systems differ, in both cases the battery charges itself—in other words, you just drive it like a regular car, no charging required. Both are also EPA and CARB Ultra Low Emissions Vehicle Certified (ULEV), meaning they're about 50 percent cleaner than the average new model year car.

It's not just individual drivers who are opting for more fuel- and emissions-efficient vehicles. FedEx has introduced the OptiFleetE700, an environmentally superior delivery truck. The new vehicle is expected to decrease particulate emissions by 96 percent, reduce smog-causing emissions by 65 percent, and travel 57 percent farther on a gallon of gas, reducing fuel costs by a third.

UPS has also introduced a fleet of 1,500 alternative-fuel delivery trucks and implemented a "no left turn" system in which deliveries are mapped out to avoid left turns, which decreases idling time at intersections for less emissions and gas consumption. With 88,000 vehicles on the road making around 15 million deliveries a day, it adds up.

Meanwhile, cities around Europe, including London, Barcelona, Stockholm, and Hamburg, are road testing the first generation of zero-emission fuel-cell buses. Even the iconic red double-decker buses of London are going green. London mayor Ken Livingstone says it's just one part of an overall aggressive plan to cut carbon emissions. "As a major city we can set an example," he says.

There are so many developments in the area of fuel efficiency, alternative fuels, and emissions control, we truly are witnessing the start of a revolution.

Our Lady Provides Green-Powered Symbolism

> *Give me your tired, your poor,*
> *Your huddled masses yearning to breathe free . . .*
> from "The New Colossus"
> Emma Lazarus, 1883

The words of poet Lazarus, engraved on Lady Liberty's pedestal, are as true today as ever—we're all breathing a bit freer now that 100 percent of the electricity that lights Miss Liberty is "green power." The statue, Ellis Island, and several other government properties in the region are part of a three-year agreement with Pepco Energies Services to purchase green power credits. The museum's air conditioning and the flood lights that shine on Miss Liberty's torch will be supplied by windmills in Pennsylvania and West Virginia.

As always, Miss Liberty provides powerful symbolism to our nation and the world.

Luckily, There's More than One Way to Skin a Cat

In February 2005, the Kyoto Treaty, the international agreement to address climate change, became law for the 141 countries that had ratified it, including all 25 nations of the European Union. The U.S. was not among those 141 countries.

"A global policy train [left] the station," wrote David Ignatius of the *Washington Post* (February 9, 2005), "without the United States even being on board, let alone serving as conductor." The treaty was flawed but, as Ignatius points out, "by disdaining Kyoto, the administration opted out of a process that might have produced a better agreement."

Less than a month after the Kyoto Treaty took effect, a group of U.S. mayors, lead by Seattle mayor Greg Nickels, came together to ask their colleagues nationwide to join the U.S. Mayors Climate Protection Agreement. By the time Nickels testified before a U.S. Senate Environment and Public

Works Committee in February 2007, he had the voices of more than 400 of his fellow mayors behind him.

The Mayors Climate Campaign 2007 makes three major requests of Congress:

- Establish a national cap on greenhouse gas emissions and a flexible market-based system of tradable allowances for emitting industries.

- Pass climate-friendly energy and transportation policies; create funding and incentives to help cities in their effort to curb emissions.

- Establish a national goal to cut emissions 80% by 2050.

In Europe, as celebrations for the 50th anniversary of the Treaty of Rome, which marked the creation of the European Union, get underway, the EU is working on a major binding commitment, going beyond the Kyoto treaty, to reduce greenhouse gas emissions by 20 percent and to increase the share of renewable energies by 20 percent.

The majority of Americans believe that the United States needs to lead, aggressively and swiftly, in the issue of climate change. Until we have that national leadership, my good news search reveals that people everywhere—from large corporations to small mom-and-pop businesses, to pockets of government like the mayors, to individuals—are waking up and taking action.

May I Suggest . . .
How We Frame the Issue Matters

It could have been just a wonky PowerPoint presentation, but what has made Al Gore's documentary *An Inconvenient Truth* so effective is that while it delivers the bad news in vivid, undeniable terms—the graphs, the icebergs, the polar bears—there's an underlying optimism in the presentation that inspires us to take heart and take action. (How many of you who saw it immediately took the action of telling others to see it, too?) Gore and the film communicate that, yes, this is an enormous issue, perhaps the biggest one yet faced by humankind, but there's already a lot being accomplished and, with the right attitude and action, we can meet the challenge. Thought translates into action. By changing our consciousness about the Earth and our relationship to it, we act accordingly, in small ways and large, and the world changes.

How we frame issues, how we think about them, is important. What we name them matters, too, because the name points our minds and imaginations in a particular direction. "The fight against global warming" becomes a mantra, and our minds are focused on a "fight" and on the problem, "global warming." In other words, we use our collective energy counterproductively when we're focused on what we *don't* want rather than focusing on what we *do* want.

So, the challenge: Can anybody out there—maybe you?— think of a positive, solutions-based term to replace "the fight against global warming." Let's get creative and come up with something vivid and positive—then spread it like a virus.

Epilogue

Changing Minds, Changing Paradigms

ep-i-logue

noun / a concluding section that rounds out the design of a book or other written work • a speech addressed to the audience by an actor at the end of a play • the final scene of a play that comments on or summarizes the main action • concluding section of a written work often dealing with the future of its characters

---

Now don't you feel better after all that good news, more informed and inspired? Don't you feel motivated to do something good for the world, or even just for your friends and family? That's what good news does. We have such an abundance of resources in this world—money, brains, creativity. Imagine what it would be like if more of us used these resources for the larger good and encouraged each other to do so, too.

As for the news itself, what if we went on a News Diet? Let's take care of our minds the way we take care of our bodies. When we pursue a balanced, healthy diet, we pay attention to the quality and quantity of food we consume. Now let's consider the quality and quantity of news we consume.

We can start by simply being aware. What are we reading, watching, and listening to? Are we contributing to the bad news environment by spreading it ourselves? When we're talking with others, are we focused on the negative? If so, let an *And Now for the Good News* alarm sound in our minds and ask, Are we gaining anything constructive from this information? If not, it's time to shift our minds, and mouths, to another topic.

Throughout this book, we've seen how individual changes in thinking can become trends in our collective awareness. What was once considered normal can become unacceptable, even abhorrent, to us. The issue of smoking provides a vivid illustration of how a paradigm can shift, dramatically and seemingly overnight. It's hard to imagine today, but just a few years ago, when we flew from coast to coast, we sat in a smoke-filled cabin, the guy sitting next to us lighting up whenever he pleased . . .

Smoking on a Plane

In the early 1900s, smoking jackets and hats were the rage and cigarettes were a part of life. By World War II, the U.S. government was supplying its soldiers with cigarette rations and Bette Davis starred in perhaps her most popular film, *Now, Voyager*, in which leading man Paul Henreid takes two cigarettes from his pack, lights both in his mouth, and offers one of them to Davis. Audiences went wild for the scene; it was perceived as romantic, even erotic. (Watching it today, we can hardly keep from laughing, it seems so absurd.)

When I was growing up in the '60s and '70s, my parents smoked. So did nearly all their friends. They always talked about quitting—didn't like being dependent on cigarettes, didn't like the physical effects, felt guilty about the expense. They were getting ready for a change.

It took a while. In 1964, when the first major U.S. report on smoking and health was published and concluded that cigarette smoking and lung cancer were linked, it didn't have an immediate impact on my parents' relationship with cigarettes or with the general public's either; they continued to smoke in restaurants, on planes, pretty much everywhere. Few non-smokers thought to complain because it was so normal—it was *just the way things were.*

But quietly, over time, events and attitudes were converging until, in what seemed like a sudden shift, we reached the tipping point.

"The tipping point"—the wonderfully descriptive phrase made popular by Malcolm Gladwell's bestselling book (Little, Brown, 2002)—comes from epidemiology and refers to the moment when a virus or disease reaches critical mass. Gladwell uses the term to refer to the moment when an idea or phenomenon gains enough momentum to hit us like a virus and spread through the masses. That's what happened with smoking.

Reports of lung cancer in people who didn't smoke became more and more common until we were all familiar with the phrase "passive smoke." Bars and restaurants began installing air filters. The insurance industry found itself paying out on policies for expensive cancer treatments. Tobacco companies' efforts to make cigarettes even more addictive were exposed and lawsuits were filed. As a result of this individual, societal, and economic convergence, we were coming to view smoking in a new way.

Once we began to question what we had taken for granted, we "magically" transformed from a society in which smokers ruled to one in which smokers were relegated to special smoking areas, then later denied smoking areas at all, until whole cities declared themselves nonsmoking areas.

A few years ago, if someone had said that pubs in Ireland would be "going nonsmoking," we'd have laughed. But they did.

- Most people smoke, and they smoke anywhere they want; that's just the way it is.

- Some people in the world don't have enough clean water or food to eat; that's just the way it is.

- We're harming the environment beyond repair; that's just the way it is.

- Humans war with one another; that's just the way it is.

If more and more of us can imagine that things can be better than "just the way it is," eventually we'll reach the tipping point. Famine, global warming, war—they'll seem just as absurd as lighting up on a plane.

I'm an optimist. I believe we're in the midst of an awakening regarding news and how it affects us. Some of us are aware that we need a change. Some news outlets, too, are starting to move away from the all-bad-news-all-the-time formula. If we encourage them, we'll wake up one day to find that the tone of our favorite news source is intelligently inquiring and solutions-oriented; we'll hear about the challenges we face and also about the important achievements we've made. And it will transform us.

New paradigms start with the individual. You and me.

op-ti-mism

noun / hopefulness and confidence about the future or the successful outcome of something • an inclination to put the most favorable construction upon actions and events or to anticipate the best possible outcome • a doctrine that this world is the best possible world • the belief that the universe is improving and that good will ultimately triumph

Moment Point Press
publisher of books that help us all
consciously create limitless lives
in a limitless world